ISBN-10: 1936463997
ISBN-13: 9781936463992

OPEN THROUGH THE MINDFLOW

Copyright 2011 John Reeves

Photos:
Cover & back cover by Rodger Brown
Portrait by Marissa Kaiser
Graphic Design by Matt Savoury

On the cover art + design:

"We all look at screens. We all view screens daily. I see the Etch A Sketch screen as a vintage digital screen. I would also say that about 75-80% of our lives is spent viewing screens. In this digital age screen viewing is running rampant via our cell phones, computers, and televisions. I see my cover art as a homage to screens, old and new. The back cover art, titled *Framed Viola*, is an original mixed media sculpture."

-

Come visit us on the web!

Shook Up Publishing
www.shookup.com

Notice of Rights
All rights reserved.
Published in the United States by Shook Up Publishing. No part of this book may be reproduced or transmitted in any form by any means, electronic, mechanical, recording or otherwise, without the prior written permission of the publisher. For information on getting permission for reprints contact info@shookup.com.

Catalog # 1007

INTRO

OPEN THROUGH THE MINDFLOW is a collection of poetry, lyrics, drawings, paintings, and short stories created by John Reeves over the last decade. This body of work is a labor of love and self expression. These words, and compilations of art were conceived while living in San Diego, California, Portland, Oregon, and New York, New York spanning over more than ten years of time. Mostly spontaneous, the art within the pages of this book are heartfelt comments on living and life as the author sees it.

John Reeves currently resides in Brooklyn, New York.

Please enjoy and don't forget to
OPEN THROUGH THE MINDFLOW...

CONTENTS

I. POEMS

2:51 AM
AFFECTION
ANATHEMA
ARTIFICIAL TEARS
BLACK TEARS
BOSUM
BREAD ON THE TABLE
BUKOWSKI
CANNOT LIVE
CATS AND DOGS
CONSEQUENCES
CRUMBLE
DIABLERIE
EXCESSIVE DESIRE
EVEN THE UGLY ONES
FUCK YOU, PEACE
HARNESS THE GET
HELL YES KIDS
IN THE CORNER
JESUS WITH A NIGHTSTICK
LET THEM BE KIDS
MORNING LADIES
NO HAY BANDO
ON THE WAGON
RULES
ROMPERS
SERIOUS
SMART PEOPLE
SPONTANEITY
THE FLOAT
THE UNIVERSE
THERE
TRUST FUND MISSION
THEY ARE ALL, "THE MAN"

II. LYRICS

A MAN SHOULD CRY
ABDUCTED
ADVENTURERS
ALIBIS
ASK DA CREATAH
BALANCE
BEAUTY
BLACK BELT IN HEAVEN
CAN'T ASK
COVET
DA ACTION HIT
D.M.F.
DOUBTS
END OF THE WORLD (I WILL LIVE)
EXPLOSION
FALLEN HEROES
FAT FUN FLOLM FEEL
FEEL
GOD RIDE
GOLD
HATED THAT GUY
HEAVY LIFE
iDRANK2MUCH
I'M QUITTIN' YOU
IS IT A GOD
IT'S DRAINING ME
IT'S LEOPARD
LIARS
LIFEFORM
LION
MY FLOW
NOBODY'S HOME
ONE DAY HELL
POP OFF

LYRICS *(cont.)*

PRIVATE THINGS
ROOM OF GLASS
SCREAM & HOLLA
SEFUCTRESS
SHE'S SO SWEET
SHIT DON'T MATTER IN SD
SHOOT THE MOON
SLINKY
SOCIAL SCENE
SOUPERMAN
STAYIN' SANE
SUNNY'S HAPPY SONG
THE TRUTH IS MINE
TIME IS NOW
WHAT'S IT REALLY WORTH
YOU CAN LOVE
YOU COME UP

III. LISTS

   A. DEATH OR RESPONSIBILITY
       1. GRADUATE
       2. DEATH MASK
       3. A BOY AND HIS DOG
       4. SLIPPIN' MICKEY
       5. DEATH OR RESPONSIBILITY

   B. PENCIL LINES
       1. GO KISS A DUCK
       2. BEARS AND SQUIRRELS
       3. CIRCLE OF LIFE
       4. I'M STILL SUING
       5. RETURN THE MONEY
       6. TECHNO BIRD
       7. PIERCED LOVE
       8. OODLES OF NOODLES
       9. BODEGA BIRD GANG
       10. AM I GOING TO DIE
       11. ROUND STONES

   C. QUOTES

   D. THE BAGGIE SERIES
       1. REAL BLOOD
       2. TEAR
       3. I.N.I = REAL PERSON
       4. GRIPFACE
       5. CAT-EYE SHOULDER GUYS
       6. BUMPFACE
       7. MATCHSTICKFACE

LISTS *(cont.)*

    E. THE BLACK NAIL PROJECT
         1. BLACK PINKY
         2. BANQUET BEER
         3. COMI
         4. WATCH VAGINA
         5. BELT VAGINA
         6. BACK TO LONDON
         7. AS I AM
         8. UMBRELLA SMOKE

IV. SHORTS

    3 WISHES
    DEATH FUNNY PAPERS AND VAPORS
    MAGICAL MINI-BAR BOTTLE OF JAMESON
    ME BAD
    SEAMLESS RAREBIT & THE BEACH CHICKENS
    THE BLUE ROCKET
    THE SILENCE IS KILLING ME
    UPTOWN SCENARIO
    WHERE THE WORMS GO TO DIE
    WHITE SANDS MOTEL

POEMS

2:51 AM

Two fifty one AM what's heard?
Two fifty one AM who lurks?
Two fifty one AM who works?
Two fifty one AM who plays?
Two fifty one AM who stays?

Only the fryers are left.
Mike what's fire?
Oh it's only the blue unicorn.
To take all who try it.
Way out of the norm.
Make you run around as if you were unborn.
Make you stay up all night looking at porn.

Two fifty one AM what's heard?
Two fifty one AM who lurks?
Two fifty one AM who works?
Two fifty one AM who plays?
Two fifty one AM who stays?

Just stay up till daylight because it's just around the bend.
Another whole new day awaits to do it all over again.

affection.

There is a difference between just being
 and really living.

Affection.
I can go on that.

I'm not depressed.
I can go on that.

I am not useless.
Affection.

Redemption.
I can go on that.

anathema.

Anathema is how I feel.
An anathema and it is so real.

You think you're close when you try to talk.
Only having thoughts shot back in your heart.

Being an anathema is a critical blow.
It is possible to re-grow, just so you know.

Shot out, discarded and forgotten.
The anathema feels this and the very bottom.

That is, until the anathema can go to the garden.
The garden where one feels enheartened.

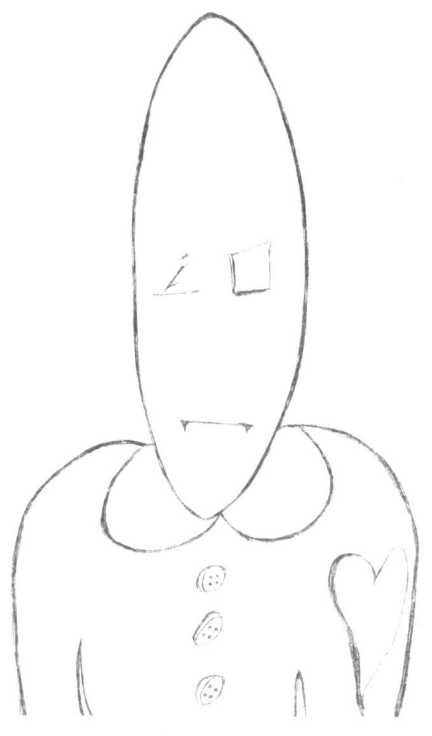

artificial tears.

The elephant drops
Those huge raindrops
The kind that flood stadium parking lots
The kind that flood rooms and entire apartments
You ask what's wrong, you get complete silence
And then the complete silence turns into complete violence
Intolerable water that consumes
Even the strongest alliance
And when the tide recedes
The calmness cleanses all tyrants

The elephant drop rips
Those huge raindrops scare
You ask questions to be completely aware
Then the artificial tears turn into complete violence
An intolerable water that consumes
Even the strongest alliance
When the tide recedes
The calmness still cleanses all tyrants

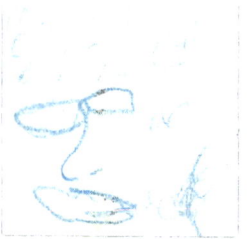 

DRUNK INJUNS

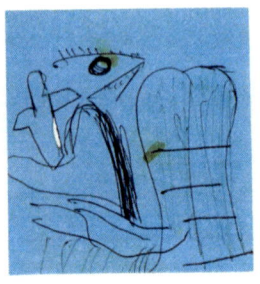 

BLACK TEARS

POST IT'S...AS IT WERE.

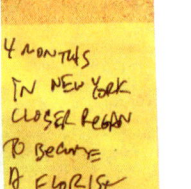 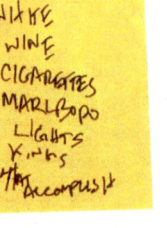 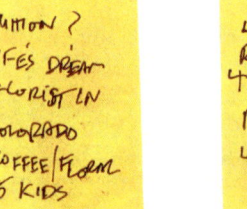

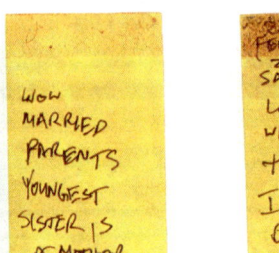 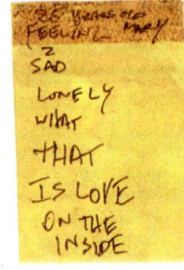 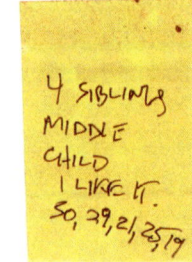

- 4 MONTHS IN NEW YORK CLOSER REGAN TO BECOME A FLORIST FLOWER SCHOOL NY

- HATE WINE CIGARETTES MARLBORO LIGHTS KINDS WHAT ACCOMPLISH

- TUITION? LIFE'S DREAM FLORIST IN COLORADO COFFEE/FLORAL 5 KIDS

- LONGEST RELATIONSHIP 4 YEARS. NOT SATISFIED LONG DISTANCE

- WOW MARRIED PARENTS YOUNGEST SISTER IS A MOTHER

- 25 YEARS OLD FEELING MOODY SAD LONELY WHAT THAT IS LOVE ON THE INSIDE

- 4 SIBLINGS MIDDLE CHILD I LIKE IT. 30, 29, 21, 25, 19

- GREELY, CO COUNTRY COW TOWN LIVED 2 TOGETHER

black tears.

Drunk Injuns.
Black Tears.
Post, "As it were."

4 months in New York.
Closer to Reagan.
To become a florist.
Flower school NY.

White wine, cigarettes, Marlboro Lights.
Kings what accomplish?
Tuition?
Life's dream florist in Colorado.
Coffee/floral shop, 5 kids.
Longest relationship 4 years.
Not satisfied, long distance.
WOW! Married parents.
Youngest sister is a mother.
25 years old feeling Mary.
2 sad 2 lonely what that?
Is love on the inside?
4 siblings middle child.

I like it.
30, 29, 25, 21, 19.
Greely, CO country cow town.
Lived two together.

bosum.

But this is a big city.
S.D. is small, but growing.
Don't tell me. Bosum.
Tell you.
Your story, unless I ask.
I am not rocking no voluntary.
Not to be cool.
Not to be popular.
To share, just so people know.
I'm a good, cowboy good Lord.
Just my jeans, seen?
Then I woke up and it was just OK.

bread on the table.

Bread on the table is everything.
Bread on the table is diamond rings.
Bread on the table is social bliss.
Bread on the table is hit don't miss.

You can have it all.
However,
if you do not know you and who you are,
Then having it all means nothing.
Knowing who you are means having it all.
Including the bread on the table.

Bread on the table is everything.
Bread on the table is diamond rings.
Bread on the table is social bliss.
Bread on the table is hit don't miss.

cannot live.

No one is near so forget about it.
Everyone's clear so forget about it.
Everything's clear don't forget about it.
This beat is here don't forget about it.
No one is near don't forget about it.
Your love is clear don't forget about it.
Everything's fun so forget about it.
Everything's numb that's why I live without it.
All life gets numb so live without it.
Nobody's home so forget about it.
I'm all alone so forget about it.
Everything's fun you better scream and shout it.

Bukowski.

Please do not judge.
Please do not judge me.
Please do not judge all black people.
Please do not judge all black people on my behavior.

For, I.
For, I pattern.
For, I pattern my life.
For, I pattern my life after a white man.

That is, at this point in my life. I don't know if it will be forever.
After a white man, that goes by the name of "Bukowski."
That is not entirely true.
Some aspects are *the bulletproof truth.*

Bukowski must be alive.
Bukowski is alive.
I deliver mail on time.
Bukowski is a friend of mine.

Since cats & dogs & dogs & cats, are all over the world. plus living in HARMONY in many countries and almost on ALL continents, if not all. I guess there are cats & dogs on all continents. I know that cats & dogs are in many civilizations, surviving without no more conflict than a chase. Why cannot man? WHY cannot woman? Why can not HUMAN? Why can't WOMEN & MEN? without conflict? I see some of the answer in & of this it is...
MONEY, CAPITAL, AND COMPETITION.
...aardvark -

cats and dogs.

Since cats and dogs and dogs and cats are all over the world, living in harmony in many countries and on most continents... Why cannot man?

Cats and dogs are living in many civilizations surviving without conflict. We must admit that cats and dogs have no more conflict than a mere chase... Why cannot woman?

Why cannot human?
Why cannot women and men? Why cannot men and women?

Without conflict?
When I look at cats and dogs and dogs and cats...

I see the answer as some of this...
It is money, capital, and competition.

In our society these things equal power.
Power abused everyday.

Money, capital, and competition.

CADAVER DOGS!

VEGAN CARNIVORE OR YOUR FAVORITE MEAL

commode

SADIE DOG.

REGURGITATION

I might show vomit.
I might scratch this.
I sing chain reptile vomit.
I like a broken record does
I stay not to regurgitate

sins of dog laws

THREATS ONLY
MAKE THE
REBEL MORE
REBELLIOUS
lay down your own

consequences.

Just like the birds sing...
Just like the birds chirp...
In this life there must be consequences.

Just like the birds sing...
Just like the birds chirp...
There must be consequences.

In this life, in this life, there are consequences!

Just like the birds sing...
Just like the birds chirp...
In this life there must be consequences.

Just like the birds sing...
Just like the birds chirp...
There must be consequences.

In this life, in this life, there are consequences!

crumble.

YO! I got too many problems in my life.
Man, can you understand this?

I said I got too many problems in my life so worrying about,
hours and shit?
Man, I'm trying to put these hours in…

I feel like all they're doing is taking hours out.
I feel like they are taking hours out of my life!

And it's only causing me more strife.
I need to make these hours count for something.

Like, build towards a better something...
I need to be optimistic on this shit.

I can't even keep hating this shit.
Or it's all going to come down to a crumble.

And then I won't even be able to talk...
I'll just mumble.

I don't want it all to come down to this crumble.
Because, I know that I can talk...

I don't just mumble.

diablerie.

I can't believe you'd leave me like this.
I cannot fathom in my wildest imagination
that you would leave me like this.
On the worst possible week of my life.
You said 3 days.
When my face was ripe.
Beaten to a pulp on the left side.
Not to mention my lost pride.
Or the knots and bumps on the right.

You must have met some gracious host.
Gone a whole week when I needed you most.
It would not be as bad if you would respond.
I tried to contact you all night long.
You say you love, but you are wrong.
Love is an unconditional moan.
If you loved then you'd be home.

excessive desire.

Dollar. Pound. Yen. Euro.

$. £ . ¥ . € .

Dollar. Pound. Yen. Euro.

$. £ . ¥ . € .

Currency.

EXCESSIVE DESIRE LEADS TO MISERY.

even the ugly ones.

Not to say that there are any...
Ugly ones, that is.

Most have some sense of beauty.
Most have some sense of kindness...

I see it daily.

The beauty.
The kindness.

Inherent in each one...
Permanent in all varieties...

Only if this could be so clear
To all of society.

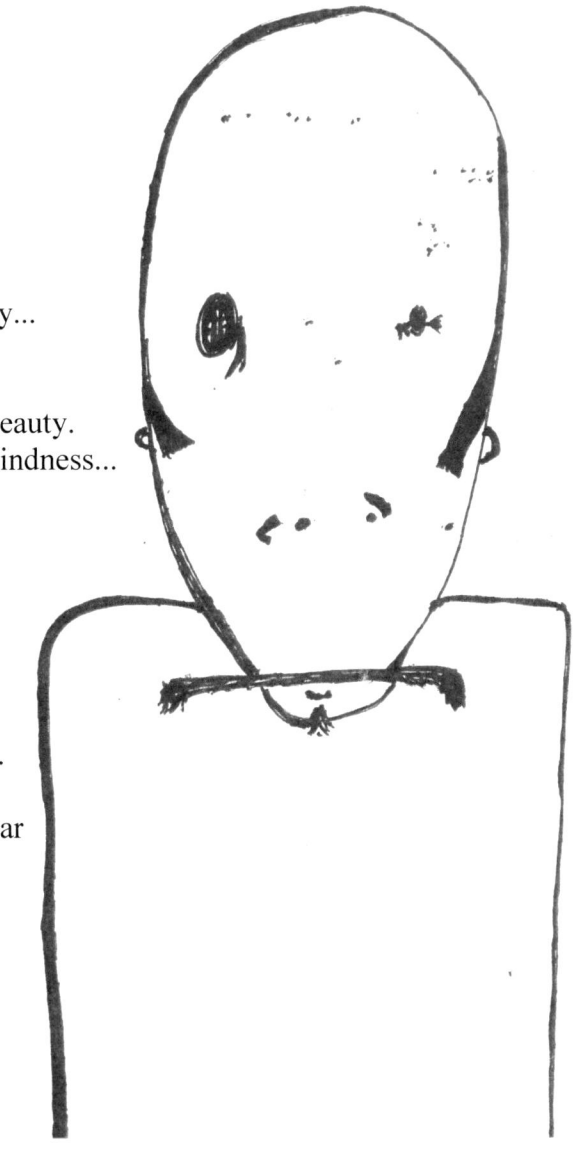

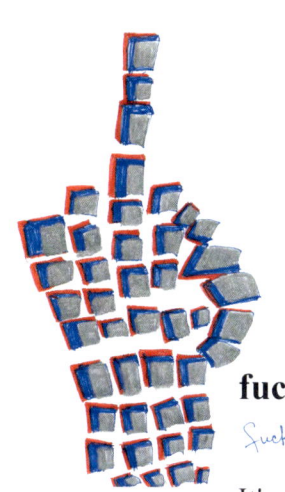

fuck you, peace.

It's not like FUCK YOU! PEACE!
it's like fuck you, peace.

It's not like FUCK YOU! PEACE!
it's like fuck you, peace.

It's not like FUCK YOU! PEACE!
it's like fuck you, peace.

*Instead of anarchy. It's like fuck you, peace.
Because if someone is coming to you in a...*

*so to speak,
with some kind of negative energy
or in a bad way
You would just say, fuck you, peace.*

It's not like FUCK YOU! PEACE!
it's like fuck you, peace.

harness the get.

If one cannot harness the get,
then one loses quality.

Dogs will bark,
fleas will cling,
and cats will pounce.

Although if one does not,
harness the get,
then they will see none of this.

And as a result,
then one will need to bounce.

HELL YES, KIDS.

Those are the ones, the ones over there.
Not the ones over here.
The ones over there.

The ones making up their own rules.
The ones that many would call a fool.
I call them the "Hell Yes, Kids."

The Hell Yes Kids...
Could be an organization, could be a fraternity...

The Hell Yes Kids could be an imagination.
The Hell Yes Kids could be a hallucination.
The Hell Yes Kids are true.
The Hell Yes Kids are the ones who knew.

The ones who are smart.
The ones who know how to treat life as art.

The Hell Yes Kids always say, "SWEET!"
Even if sometimes their future looks bleak.

in the corner.

In the corner by the door
Is a pretty good spot
In the corner by the door
It doesn't get too hot

In the middle... is the riddle
You ask yourself
Why is it so hot?

Because in the middle
Too many mingle and breathe
And what not...

In the middle... is the riddle
Do you think not?

In the corner...
By the door...
Is a pretty good spot.

jesus with a nightstick.

Jesus with a nightstick.
Jesus with a nightstick righting wrongs.
Jesus with a nightstick righting wrongs all night long.
Correcting ill corrections with his songs.
And words that most humans tend to rely on.

Words that most humans try to live by.
The words that most humans use to try to survive.

Jesus with a nightstick all night long...
You really think you are Jesus with your badge and gun.
Always trying to wreck somebody's fun.
Out on the street, thinking you're number one.

Jesus with a nightstick all night long...
Even if you have power do not abuse it.
Plus, please don't hit people with your nightstick!
The ones with heart will learn this shit.

JESUS WITH A NIGHTSTICK IS LEGIT.

let them be kids.

Let them be kids
Let them learn
Let them earn
In life you get burned
Even if it is not deserved
Some lives get burnt
Next life they'll learn
Everything is earned
Love life don't hurt
The things we want
We should earn
Love life don't burn
Let them be kids
Let them love
And love to learn

morning, ladies.

I say morning ladies, even though it is afternoon.
I say morning ladies, not to be rude.
I say morning ladies with respect.
I say this...

Even though sometimes I get nil respect.
The thing that is here to address...
Is to let them know that I have respect.
I say morning ladies, with intellect.
With no response I'll still respect...
The morning ladies must repent.

Only them and God...
Know their lives
And how last night was spent.

no hay bando.

No hay bando. I have no band.
Segments man.
Farm gold.
Six-shooter.
Eleven matador.
Roll the dice.
Educated animal.
Calligraphy.
Me as a hyena.
Yeah, segments man.
No hay bando. I have no band.

on the wagon.

It's hard to be sober.
It's hard to be sober or on the wagon.
It's hard to be on the wagon and sober
when most of your heroes were not.

Hendrix, Morrison, Kennison.
Hendrix, Morrison, Kennison.

All as high as the sun.
All had so much fun, when they had fun.

Hendrix, Morrison, Kennison.
Hendrix, Morrison, Kennison.

All scholars, all users.
All dead, yet I still look to them.
All scholars, all users, all live forever.

Especially in eyes that love and admire.
What I admire is the way they spoke to life.
Even when they were tired.
Each and every one of them never retired.

rules?

Rules! What rules? Your rules? Society's rules?
Just abide. Abide by what?
Abide by the laws and rules that were set up,
millenniums ago?

Who is to say what's right? Who is to say what's wrong?
Right. Wrong. Black. White.
These colors bleed.

These colors bleed into each other until they form a beautiful,
magnificent color.
And with that color, we shall grow.
Grow to the highest of highs.

With this growth we will determine and interpret life...
in all of its meanings.
Substance, substance plus matter.
What is the matter?

Is that not the question?
Things happen, people live, and most rules are forgotten.

rompers.

Rompers! UHHH!!!
Rompers! Rompers!

Oh man those girls.
Summer girls in rompers.
Summer girls anytime, but summer girls in rompers...

OHHH! So are so on time!
Summer girls in rompers, summer girls are always on time.
Some are girls in rompers but summer girls in jeans are just fine.

serious?

Seriousness is serious.
Funniness is funny.

These kids think both are the same.
And are they?

So magnificent, is the question of whether or not?

Drama and comedy?
Are the same or not?

Can you laugh about it?
Well, if you can then it is funny.

Regardless.

WHEN TO FROWN?
WHEN TO SMILE?
THIS IS SERIOUS.

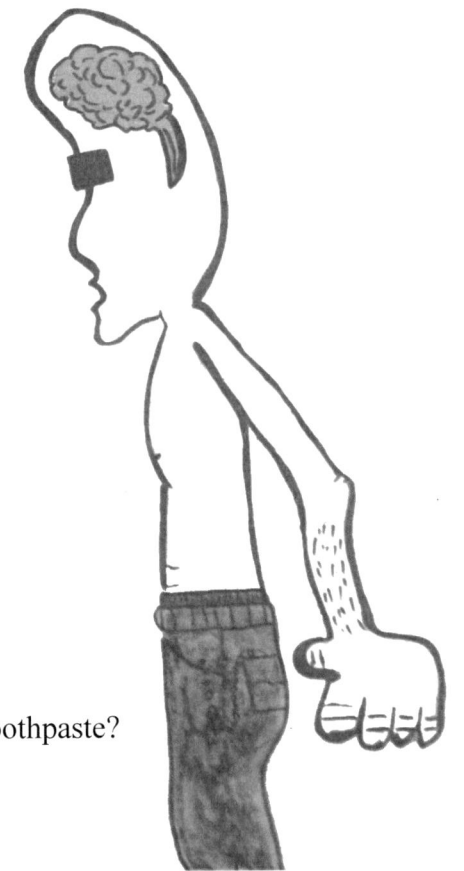

smart people.

Are you serious?
Did you just wash your body with toothpaste?

Smart people ask questions.
Smart people know answers.

Ask a smart person something, they will tell you an answer.
This does not necessarily mean said answer is true...

It just means that they are smart enough to tell you an answer what to do.
Or it means at least they are smart enough to tell you an idea what is new.

Smart people can curb your knowledge appetite.
Smart people can tell you what's right.

spontaneity.

Are you willing to try something new?
Will spontaneity be the road that you choose?

Or will stagnation take you to your tomb?
Because you cannot move;
Even though you have the room.

The will, the way, the know how,
Yet you still stay?
They want freedom is what people say.

And then they build walls like a penitentiary...
You must move in this life somehow.
To show that you know and that you are proud.

Spontaneity will give you this gift,
So please don't hesitate to take a lift.

the float.

The float. It floats.
Will it submerge?
Or will it keep its breath and stay above?

I needed payroll, that's what it was.
The second mouse refused to quit.
So it rose above.

Trouble? So it was.
Just deal with things.
Never give up.

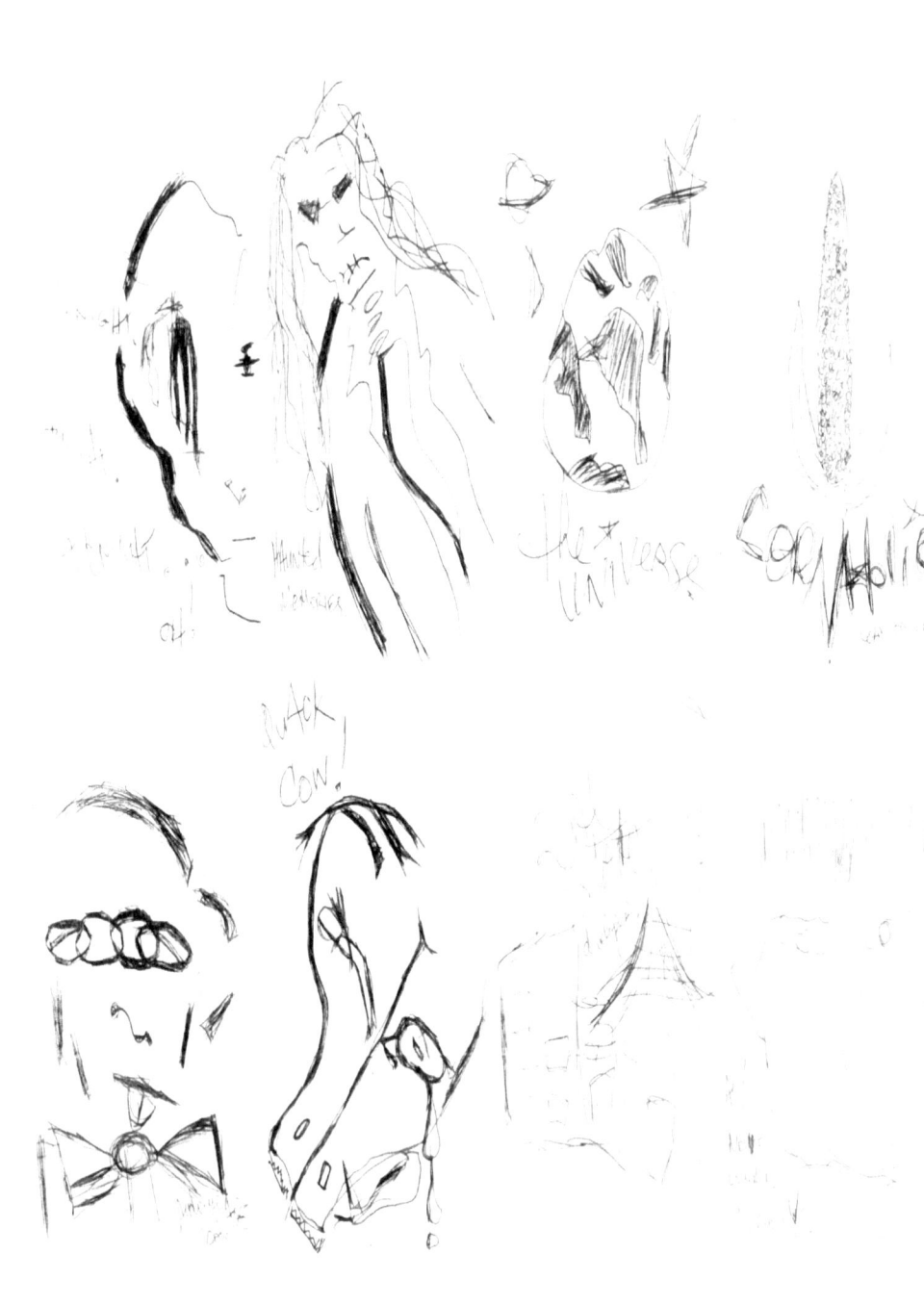

the universe.

Tonight, Tonight, Tonight, OH!
Haunted memories.
The universe.
Cornholio. On the cob.
Audi-eye bow-tie.
Quack Cow!
Real Estate Developer.
Any movie with me is funny.
This doesn't have any logical references!
Bullshit Cowpie!
Some desire.
Look---------> I've got a fridge full of beers!
China is amazing.

there.

For some it is the getting there.
For some others it is the being there.
For some are utterly and completely already there.

Where, you ask?

"There," I answer and say, "If you were *there* then you would not have to ask."
"There," is not necessarily a physical place.

It could be a state of mind or being that you feel.
It might be a level of acceptance that employs one to be still and know.

Yes ask, yes ask questions when you don't know the answer.

Although I sense that if you dig a bit deeper,
and think before you ask,

then you will tell yourself the answer.

For some it is the getting there.
For some others it is the being there.
For some are utterly and completely already there.

Where, you ask?

"There," I answer and say, "If you were *there* then you would not have to ask."

they are all, "the man."

When you live and you live deep,
You could be called the man.

When you breathe, and you breathe deep,
You could be called the man.

When you treat others how you would to like to be treated,
Then and only then...

You *should* be called the man.

No matter which prisoner of life you are,
If your actions are true...

Then and only then, you will be the man.

trust fund mission.

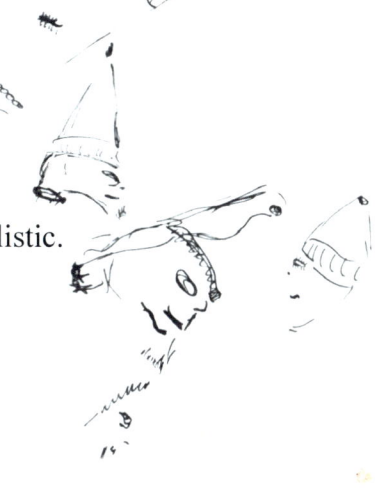

On a trust fund mission…

Some of us are so ready, so ready...
So ready to die.

Some of us are so ready, so ready...
So ready to live.

Most of us are so competitive.
Most of us are so antagonistic, so materialistic.

So ready for more.

Ready for more excess.
Ready for the next order of business.
Ready to go make that cream.
Ready to get that treat.
Ready to make them funds.

Truth is, we should all have to earn our own dividends.

LYRICS

a man should cry.

A man is not supposed to cry, he should

When things don't always go right it's good (2x)

He will be much stronger
He will live much longer

He will see what life means
He will build his family

He'll have dreams and visions
He won't hate religions

He'll have dreams and visions
He won't hate religions

He will see what life means
He will build his family

He'll have dreams and visions
He'll have dreams and visions

A man is not supposed to cry, he should

When things don't always go right it's good (2x)

abducted?

Abducted,
taken away.
Stolen from all you know,
and where you stay.

What could have done this to you?
Take you away?
Steal you from all you know and where you play?

Was it some sort of alien probe?
Was it some sort of alien probe?
Was it some sort of alien probe?

(bridge)

It's all over the papers yeah...
It's headline news.

You were abducted yeah...
Used as the alien fool.

Was it some sort of alien probe?
Was it some sort of alien probe?
Was it some sort of alien probe?

(bridge)

Abducted,
taken away.
Stolen from all you know,
and where you play.

              onward making progress in the snow
                on the high deserted plateau

          time one had stumbled
          and their ears those bees had bumbled

        horseback the other on foot
        rs to the end and so they shook

      on horseback the other on foot
     others to the end and so they shook

I, (eyeyeyeyeyeeeyeyeye) gotta take another look
and see across the mellow brook

I got to take another look and see the mellow brook

YEAH!
OH YEAH!

One on horseback the other on foot
Brothers to the end and so they shook

One on horseback the other on foot
Brothers to the end and so they shook

(BRIDGE)

One on horseback the other on foot
Brothers to the end and so they shook

One on horseback the other on foot
Brothers to the end and so they shook

I, (eyeyeyeyeyeeeyeyeye) I gotta take another look

alibis.

I'm tired of the lies and the alibis
Makin' people scream
Make 'em wanna cry
Livin' in this place is just Bed-Stuy
All this fuckin' junk makes me wanna die

But when I think of you I feel so alive (8x)

I never wanna go to beddy bye
When you talk to me you don't have to lie
I'm an open book and I do or die
So c'mon sweet baby just gimme a try

I don't wanna have to ask your friends
Where the hell you've been
Where the hell you been?
Where the hell you been?

I'm tired of the lies and the alibis
Makin' people scream
Make 'em wanna cry
Livin' in this place is just like Bed-Stuy
All this fuckin' junk makes me wanna die

But when I think of you I feel so alive (8x)

ask da creatah.

I don't know, Je suis pas, I don't know.
What's in store?
Is it new world order?

Ask the creator. (2x)

ASK THE CREATOR...

Hey Yo shit's unclear, the future's uncertain.
The future's definitely uncertain.

(peep this shit)

Hey YO times is hard, yeah it's real rough.
Niggas bombin' and lootin' not givin' a fuck.
Lyin' and cheatin' man I'm fed up!
To the brim like a Folger's coffee cup.

You need to figure it out.
What it's all about.
Are you a man or a louse plannin' shit out?
Because the future is now in this burnt out house.
While you're sittin' there ass naked on the couch.

In this cold ass world you got to plan ahead.
Cause the way shit is going I'm walking dead.
Dead man walking, man walking dead.
Trying to kill the thirteen voices in my head.
No wonder why I'm feelin' so mislead.
I gotta medicate just to go to bed.

(cont.)

Man, try to get some sleep.
I ain't here to preach.
But I aim to teach.
And purchase my own beach.
With a nice girl who tastes like a peach.

Or a plum, I'm gonna have her sprung.
On the dilz cause you know that I am very hung.
And I'm the boss of the clit with my tongue.
JTMR looks out for number one.

Man, I ain't here to preach.
But I aim teach.
And purchase an island and chill on the beach.
Man, I ain't here to preach.
But I aim to teach.
And purchase an island and chill on the beach.
Straight chillin' on the beach!

Yo the future's uncertain.
I'm just trying to get a clearer picture y'all
I don't know, Je suis pas, I don't know
What's in store?

Is it new world order?

Ask the creator. (4x)

balance.

Balance, it's something everybody needs in these days and times;
it's a new century man you can't deny. Mad chaotic episodes...
but you must try to keep that balance so you can survive.

Equality, poise, symmetry, balance
Everyone needs it, it makes life a challenge

Equality, poise, symmetry, balance
Everyone needs it, it makes life a challenge

Equality, poise, symmetry, balance
Everyone needs it, it makes life a challenge

Equality, poise, symmetry, balance
Everyone needs it, it makes life a challenge

What I need is something to go along with it
Like this clean-ass groove so that I can kick-it

Deep bass lines and some clean guitar
MCA's drum tracks always up to par

Keepin' it on the level monotonous
Hearin' it in your ear without no difference

No other style is to equivalence
So when Ya hear this

Ya betta get your balance.

Equality, poise, symmetry, balance
Everyone needs it, it makes life a challenge

Equality, poise, symmetry, balance
Everyone needs it, it makes life a challenge

Equality, poise, symmetry, balance
Everyone needs it, it makes life a challenge

Equality, poise, symmetry, balance
Everyone needs it, it makes life a challenge

Ya need that balance to stay alive
Ya need that balance to stay alive

(cont.)

Ya need that balance to stay alive
Ya need that balance to stay alive

If you're not on it you'll surely drop
Balance is what you need up to the mark

If you start to teeter take a big step

To the left or right
Catch your breath right?

Cause it's a long way to the top and you can see it
So keep Ya balance so you can achieve it

Keep your PMA just like HR say...

Yeah I'm kickin' it in the Mecca!
M-E-C-C-A the wrecka!

I don't care what you say now cause I gonna
ROCK-ROCK-ROCK
The crowd.

Positive black man you know I'm proud
Guaranteed to make your girl scream loud

And I keep the balance no doubt
And I keep the balance no doubt
And I keep the balance no doubt
And I keep the balance...

Equality, poise, symmetry, balance
Everyone needs it, it makes life a challenge

Equality, poise, symmetry, balance
Everyone needs it, it makes life a challenge

Equality, poise, symmetry, balance
Everyone needs it, it makes life a challenge

Equality, poise, symmetry, balance
Everyone needs it, it makes life a challenge

beauty.

Everybody sees what you're gonna be
Everybody sees your beauty!

Stepping on the scene
You're coming out clean

Everybody sees your beauty!
Discovering things, you're living out dreams

Everybody sees your beauty!

YOU'RE BEAUTY! (4x)

Sliding down the poles
Playing all the roles

Everybody sees your beauty!

Working overtime
Watching every dime

Everybody sees your beauty!

Getting what you need
Planting all the seeds

Everybody sees your beauty!

YOU'RE BEAUTY! (4x)

Everybody sees what you're gonna be
Everybody sees your beauty!

Stepping on the scene
You're coming out clean

Everybody sees your beauty!
Discovering things, you're living out dreams

Everybody sees your beauty!

YOU'RE BEAUTY! (4x)

black belt in heaven.

Horrible words for you...
I've got a horrible story to tell you.
As for the rape charge Kobe responds.
Man Michael Jackson guilty innocence.
Whoa O.J. Simpson the glove didn't fit!

Horrible words for you...

I've got a horrible story to tell you. (2x)

Man Mr. Coburn, what's up with him? Hitting on Kelly.
His first born son is dead!
He was my nephew; we could have been friends.
A martial artist, I took him surfing.
Too young to die, he was heaven sent.
Sorry Vanessa, he was your first kid.
Too young to die. He was excellent!

Horrible words for you...

I've got a horrible story to tell you. (2x)

Indifferent doctors, should stop practicing
That meningitis, bacteria shit!
I'm sorry sister, he was your first kid.

Horrible words for you...

I've got a horrible story to tell you. (2x)

RAY ALLEN COBURN BLACK BELT IN HEAVEN!!! (4x)

can't ask?

The facts are on file
The tune is in check
How come when I see you, you look like a wreck?

I sit and watch you for awhile
Your face is blank, it's not a smile

You're going so fast, you need a blast
As for why, I cannot ask

Your skin is blue, spider webbed
Thoughts of your death are in my head

Your skin is pale! Spider webbed
THOUGHTS OF YOUR DEATH ARE IN MY HEAD!

You're in so deep
You can't get out

It makes me sad
I have to shout

But, there's nothing that I can do
Cause if you're sprung

Then you are through!
YOU ARE THROUGH!!!

Your skin is blue, spider webbed
Thoughts of your death are in my head

Your skin is pale! Spider webbed
Thoughts of your death are in my head

I tell you darling
they're in my head

Oh baby,

they're in my head...
in my head
in my head...

covet.

Look !

It's right there,
Right there in front of your face!

Wait !

See all you can,
See all you can before it's too late!

Want !

It came to you,
It came to burden your place!

Look !

It's right there,
Right there in front of your face!

Look !

It's right there,
Right there it's such a disgrace!

Wait !

See all you can,
See all you can to win the race!

Want !

It came to you,
It came to compete at high stakes!

Look !

It's right there,
Right there in front of your face!

da action hit.

This is the action hit, come get some...
You want that action shit...

It's like a shoot em' up bang bang!

ACTION BONANZA!
GET OUT MY FACE CAUSE YOU KNOW I CAN'T STAND YA!

You get body SLAMMED!
Super fly SCHNOOKED!

Flat on your back like a SUPA fly HOOKA!
I'll damage YA!

Leave you bandaged in the morgue.
With a pale white face lookin' like Boy George.

All girlish!
And you know you're gettin' squirrellish!

In the back seat of my jeep? NO!
I'll get your girl and you know I'll rock that HO's,

MEAT! It's gonna be real sweet!
And I'll meet you in the back of the street!

It don't matter if I rhyme or not.
Cause you know a mothafucka's gonna smoke all your pot.

And your girl's too.
Cause I'm gonna sport the blue.

Till the day I do or rather die?
I multiply, stay high, get high!

West coast side to the east side.
This is the action hit, come get some...

You want that action shit...

D.M.F.

You learn a lot!
I've learned a lot!
About you tonight, and it just doesn't come through.
It just doesn't shine through!
New things are discovered, lost and found.
Overwhelmed... with joy then pain.
So much till I drowned.
What I say means so much!
But I am so out of touch!
I don't see what my words,
What my words do.

You had to go to the Del Mar Fair.
(so much money at the del mar fair)
You had go to the Del Mar Fair.

You had to go to the Del Mar Fair.
(it's not funny at the del mar fair)
You had go to the Del Mar Fair.

I make you feel!
But all I know is that this pain is real!
Listenin' to all them!
I think you do it...
Just for fun!
You do it for fun!
You do it... just for fun!!!

You had to go to the Del Mar Fair!
(it's not funny at the del mar fair)
You had to go to the Del Mar Fair!

You had to go to the Del Mar Fair!
(so much money at the del mar fair)
You had to go to the Del Mar Fair!

HOWEVER!!! I REALIZE...
THAT EVERYTHING IS JUST BULLSHIT LIES!
BULLSHIT LIES!
BULLSHIT LIES!
I REALIZE EVERYTHING IS JUST BULLSHIT LIES.

doubts.

Doubts about the buddah...
You got Doubts about yourself!

Don't give into stupid...
Stupid fuckin' shit!

You just need to listen...
Listen to the gift!

All of us are given...
Life is the biggest gift!

Doubts about the buddah...
You got Doubts about yourself!

Don't give into stupid...
Stupid fuckin' shit!

Suck it up and do it...
Stop all excuses!

You know you can prove it...
And make it benefit!

*DOUBTS ABOUT THE BUDDAH,
DOUBTS ABOUT YOURSELF.*

end of the world (I will live).

I know it seems like the end of the world,
Some things feel like the end of the world,
I know it feels like it could be the end of the world,
Some things make it seem like it's the end of the world...

SEEMS LIKE IT'S THE END OF THE WORLD!
BUT, I WILL LIVE!
SEEMS LIKE IT'S THE END OF THE WORLD!

AND YOU WILL LIVE! (5x then into the funk)

I know it seems like the end of the world,
Some things feel like the end of the world,
I know it feels like it could be the end of the world,
Some things make it seem like it's the end of the world...

SEEMS LIKE IT'S THE END OF THE WORLD!
BUT, I WILL LIVE!
SEEMS LIKE IT'S THE END OF THE WORLD!

AND YOU WILL LIVE! (5x then into the funk)

I KNOW SOMETIMES IT FEELS LIKE THE END OF THE WORLD.

explosion!

Don't be playin' with that fire, you're gonna get burned!
Don't be playin' with that fire, you're gonna get burned!

Explosion!

Fire oil ink liquid combust
Implosion wreaks havoc we cannot trust
Especially when you're out in a rush
Breathing in toxins
That make you throw up *(make you throw up)*
Shrapnel flying from the inside out
Slivers of iron hurling right to your mouth
A shuriken leaves dead bodies no doubt.

Explosion!

Extinguish it, yo and repent
Make sure you know where
Your essence is spent
Cause in this life it's hard to pay rent
Not to mention
All that digital shit *(digital shit)*
Technology moves at the speed of light
And if you're caught up man,
Yeah you think you're all right
Stayin' up late every single night
Don't keep your shit that tight
Cause you need to keep it crisp
Don't hesitate to take a lift.

Don't be playin' with that fire, you're gonna get burned!
Don't be playin' with that fire, you're gonna get burned!

Explosion!

Fire oil ink liquid combust
Implosion wreaks havoc we cannot trust
Especially when you're out in a rush
Breathing in toxins
That make us throw up
Shrapnel flying from the inside out
Slivers of iron hurling right to your mouth
A shuriken leaves dead bodies no doubt.

Explosion! Explosion! Explosion! Explosion!
Explosion! Explosion! Explosion! Explosion!
Explosion! Explosion! Explosion! Explosion!

fallen heroes.

Fallen heroes equal dead soldiers...
where I come from.

Fallen heroes equal dead soldiers...
Where I come from.

Fallen heroes equal dead soldiers...
where I come from.

America eats its young...
Too much bloodshed.

Lost sons, daughters, and fathers...
where I come from.

Truth and honor is on the front lines...
where I come from.

Too bad honor does not count at the top tier…
where I come from.

Cheaters and liars start all of the battles...
where I come from.

Truth be told we should all have more honor...
where I come from.

Fallen heroes equal dead soldiers...
where I come from.

Fallen heroes equal dead soldiers...
where I come from.

Fallen heroes equal dead soldiers...
where I come from.

BECAUSE AMERICA EATS ITS YOUNG.

fat.fun.flolm.feel.

Yeah come on! Check it out now
Come on, come on check it out...

(cause it's the fat fun flolm feel)

It is the fat fun flolm feel!
It is the fat fun flolm feel!
It is the fat fun flolm feel!

Ya betta listen up and let me tell you the deal!
It's all about the "F" you see
It makes you want to get with Reeves
The sixth letter in the alphabet
When you think of it
You get all wet

Because it represents the crew, the boys
And when we're out there we make hella noise
So girls go and get your toys!
Cause when gonna bring you lots of joys
And that happiness, and that happiness, and that happiness...

It is the fat fun flolm feel!
It is the fat fun flolm feel!
It is the fat fun flolm feel!

Ya betta listen up and let me tell you the deal!

FAT FUN FLOLM FEEL!

It is the fat fun flolm feel!
it is the fat fun flolm feel!

Ya betta listen up!
Because the "F" is where it's at
JTMR and I'm black
And you know that I smoke the skunk!
Through a bong or I roll a blunt
Eatin' chicken and watermelon chunks
And you know I get the freak
The freaky funk
In the back of my truck cause it's...

fat fun flolm feel (mellow 3x)

(cont.)

Cause it's the fat fun flolm feel!
It is the fat fun flolm feel!
It is the fat fun flolm feel!

Ya betta listen up and let me tell you the deal!

FAT FUN FLOLM FEEL!

It is the fat fun flolm feel!
It is the fat fun flolm feel!

Ya betta listen up and let me tell you the deal!

(BRIDGE)

You see that ROGIN = VYB = JTMR!
ROGSTAR up to par in the back of my car!
It is the Jimmy GMC with the 2.8
Engine! Because I win them!
Rolling down the the BLVD of MM!!!
In THE MECCA! THE MECCA!
The place I dwell!
So all you silly suckas can just go to hell...

Cause it's the fat fun flolm feel!

It is the fat fun flolm feel!
It is the fat fun flolm feel!

Ya betta listen up and let me tell you the deal!

It is the fat fun flolm feel!
It is the fat fun flolm feel!
It is the fat fun flolm feel!

Ya betta listen up and let me tell you the deal.

RIGHT NOW RESPECT:

MLK.MECCALANDKINGS.RAS.FEEL.VYB.SPOK.SAP.HESH

feel.

What you see inside of me is not what you really know
people are crazy and I'm just so lazy

but I don't even know

What you see outside of me is not what you really know

people are crazy and I'm just so lazy
but I don't even know

FA-FA-FA FEEL!
FA- FEEL. I'm feeling it
FA-FA-FA FEEL!
FA-FA-FA FEEL!
FA- FEEL. I'm feeling it
FA-FA-FA FEEL!

What you see outside of me is not what you really know
people are crazy and I'm just so lazy

but I don't even know

What you see outside of me is not what you really know
people are crazy, I'm so lazy

I don't even know

FA-FA-FA FEEL!
FA- FEEL. I'm feeling it
FA- FA fuckin' feel!
FA-FA-FA FEEL!
FA- FEEL. I'm feeling it
FA- FA fuckin' feel!

We all see and we all feel and we all hear what we want
We take for granted what we get, what we get from our moms
That's why I…

FA-FA-FA FEEL!
FA- FEEL. I'm feeling it
FA-FA-FA FEEL!
FA-FA-FA FEEL!
FA- FEEL. I'm feeling it
FA-FA fuckin' FEEL!

god ride.

(Whistling)

God, could you ride?
God, could you ride?
God, could you ride all night?

(Whistling)

Just take it all in stride
Life is just a ride
So just live free
And learn to fly
Things are on your side
So walk tall
Head up high!

God, could you ride?
God, could you ride?
God, could you ride all night?

(Whistling)

God, could you ride?
God, could you ride?
God, could you ride all night?

Just take it all in stride
Life is just a ride
So just live free
And learn to fly
Things are on your side
So walk tall
Head up high!

(Whistling)

God, could you ride?
God, could you ride?
God, could you ride all night?

gold.

You're my gold
Piece of gold
Ready for my soul
A precious metal

(beggin' beggin' beggin' for my soul)
Something special
(beggin' beggin' beggin' for my soul)
A special special precious metal

And time don't matter
You're my gold
Your heart's on fire
You're my playground love
And time don't matter
My heart's on fire
For my precious gold
You keep on workin'
You keep on lurkin'
To find that special gold
It's my weapon
My special weapon
That's the golden love
The playground love
All official
So official
It's the playground love
Hearts on platters, hearts on platters

hated that guy.

Sometimes there are things to fight for,
And
Sometimes you can even the score;
But, I dunno why these people try to show me.
Every now and then people fuck with you,
And you know that they think they are right.
And you fight,
And you fight,
And you fight,
And fight! But you are always right!!!

I already hated that guy.
I already hated him!
I already hated that guy.
I already hated,
I hated him.

Every now and then people fuck with you,
And you know that they think they are right.
And you fight,
And you fight,
And you fight,
And fight! But you are always right!!!

I already hated that guy.
I already hated him!
I already hated that guy.
I already hated,
I hated him.

Sometimes there are things to fight for,
And
Sometimes you can even the score;
But, I dunno why these people try to tell me.
Every now and then people fuck with you,
And you know that they think they are right.
And you fight,
And you fight,
And you fight,

Let's fight! But you are always right!!!

I already hated that guy.
I already hated him!
I already hated that guy.
I already hated,
I hated him.

heavy life.

Heavy, heavy life. Heavy, heavy life.

It's so much in my heart... It's so much in my soul...
It's so much in my heart... It's so much in my soul...

Heavy, heavy life. Heavy, heavy life. Heavy, heavy life.

It's so much in my heart... It's so much in my soul...
It's so much in my heart... This heavy, heavy life.

Explore the next world, explore all over your girl.
Explore her whole world, explore your girl.

In this heavy, heavy life (4x)

It's so much in my heart... It's so much in my soul...
It's so much in my heart... It's so much in my soul...

HEAVY, HEAVY LIFE.

idrank2much.

I drank too much last night...

Drinkin'. Smokin'. Skatin'. Creatin'.
Drinkin'. Smokin'. Skatin'. Creatin'.

Oh no! Watch out here comes that party guy.
You label me an alcoholic.
Knowin' damn well I get tech like Peter Smolik.
Knowin' damn well just like Mr. Smolik,
If I drink yo it's what I call it.
Drinkin' Long Islands and Gin & Tonics.
I drink as a form of pleasure.
Relaxation is something I will always treasure.
Like a Newport it's alive with pleasure.

Power slidin' down the block and you know I rock it.
And don't even ask what's in my pocket.
OK, St. Ides, O.E., and Chronic.
You dumb ass popes need to stop it.
Causin' Reeves to check, cause you know he pop it.
And drop it and lock it.
Down stairs, gaps, and escalators.

I drank too much last night... Got bills... Got bills...

Drinkin'. Smokin'. Skatin'. Creatin'.
Drinkin'. Smokin'. Skatin'. Creatin'. (2x)

Ah me no scared of no elevators!
And I got mad respect for all y'all skaters.
And anyone who ain't no mother hater.
All my skills come from mad creators.
Some say life is just a party.
The same one who end up sayin' sorry.
UNDERSTAND THIS!
Life is a dream and a precious gift.
So rub the bottle and get your chance and get your wish.
JTMR knows all of this.

Hypocrites say that I drink too much.
Hypocrites say that I always drink too much!

i'm quittin' you.

I know all about the things you do.
You lie and you think that you can just; pull the wool,

Over my eyes, to your surprise...
I already knew. Your secrets and your lies...

I saw through to the deepest black and my attack is through.

My attack is through
My attack is few
My attack is through
I'm quittin' you.

Resisting at this point is good.
Resist to hear all of the untruths.

To spoil what I thought that I knew.
Ecstasy and love are only just for two.

The ones who understand how to live and just what to do.

My attack is through
My attack is few
My attack is through
I'm quittin' you.

I know all about the things you do.
You lie and you think that you can just; pull the wool,

Over my eyes, to your surprise...
I already knew. Your secrets and your lies...

I saw through to the deepest black and my attack is through.

My attack is through
My attack is few
My attack is through
I'm quittin' you.

is it a god?

AND HERE HE IS... DIRECT FROM THE BAR!

I'm not sayin' I'm God or nothin'...
I ain't sayin' I'm God or anything...

BUT THE BLACK MAN IS. (4x)

Original man. Pangea.
Mother Earth Africa beneath YA!
Plate tectonics. It's ironic.
How most of us rap about chronic.
But, don't even know how the world was formed.
Word is born!
I'm here to take you out from the norm.
Rollin' in like a mothafuckin' storm.

I'm not even trying to say that I'm godlike.
I'm not sayin' that I'm a higher power...

BUT THE BLACK MAN IS. (4x)

African motherland.
Queen of the Earth.
The center of Pangea for what it's worth.
The place of man and monkeys birth.
The place where Adam's ribs came out the dirt.
The place where God did all his works.
Turning water to wine and grass into herb.
What is your higher power?
Is something new every hour?
Is it a God?
Is it something that came out the fog?

Is it something you get from a bottle?
Is it something controlled by a throttle?
Is it your T.V.?
Because you can see me?
Because my life's on screen?
Is it something you get from a bottle?
Is it something controlled by a throttle?
Is it your T.V.?
Because you can see me?
Because my life's on screen?

it's draining me.

Can you fix that hole? In the bottom of the sea?
It's draining me.

It's draining so much of so many souls.
Why can't they fix that hole?

Man got technology,
Man got the space and thieves.

Man got to the moon.
Man got technology.

But will he please just cover that hole?
No more oil birds.

We don't like seeing that shit.
That shit ain't legit!

It's too much filth and dredge.
So can you just please fix that hole for us?

We don't need no more oil.
It's almost to New York now,
Louisiana, Florida, all over the gulf.

We don't want our whole seas to be filled with that shit.
So man fix the hole!

Didn't I tell you about that hole?
Didn't you lose your mind this time?

(whistling)

END.

it's leopard.

Yeah holmes did you check out that girl mang, tell me...
She said, "She wants to go home."
She said that she needed a ride home.
Yeah man, I'll take her home.
Dammit, I'll take her home.

YEAH IT'S LEOPARD ESE, YEAH IT'S LEOPARD ESE,

She had a whole full suit made of leopard...
From head to toe, it was leopard.

YOU CAN'T ARGUE WITH NO FRIENDS OF MINE!
(YOU CAN'T ARGUE WITH NO FRIENDS OF MINE!)

YOU CAN'T ARGUE WITH NO FRIENDS OF MINE!
(YOU CAN'T ARGUE WITH NO FRIENDS OF MINE!)

YOU CAN'T ARGUE WITH THE CORRECT TIME!
(YOU CAN'T ARGUE WITH THE CORRECT TIME!)

YOU CAN'T ARGUE WITH THE CORRECT TIME!
(YOU CAN'T ARGUE WITH THE CORRECT TIME!)

Yeah man, I'll take her home.
Dammit, I'll take her home.

YEAH IT'S LEOPARD ESE, YEAH IT'S LEOPARD ESE,

She had a whole full suit made of leopard...
From head to toe, it was leopard.

YOU CAN'T ARGUE WITH NO FRIENDS OF MINE!
YOU CAN'T ARGUE WITH NO FRIENDS OF MINE!

YOU CAN'T ARGUE WITH NO FRIENDS OF MINE!
YOU CAN'T ARGUE WITH NO FRIENDS OF MINE!

liars.

Liars, they live in hell
And that is where they will dwell

Honor, we strive to tell the truth
And live so that we are bulletproof

Liars, will burn in hell
Because the truth they do not tell

Liars, they shall learn the truth
They learn the truth that is bulletproof

Because if liars do not learn the truth
They will burn in hell like a dried out old boot

Liars lie, and most of them, they always cry
I'm trying not to die, I'm trying not to die

If I die I don't want to burn forever
Because that shit is not clever

Liars burn in hell
Cause what they tell

Is what the devil sells.

lifeform.

See my precious little fingers
View my toes...
See my knees you want to squeeze them
My elbows...

Play with my feet now
Shake my hands...
Give me five
Even though I don't understand!

Some precious lifeform
Watch it grow
When it stops you'll never know

Some precious lifeform
Watch it grow
When it stops you'll never know
You'll never know...

Throw me up and down
Swing my arms...
Do your best not to give me any harm

Play with my feet now
Shake my hands...
Give me five
Even though I don't understand!

Some precious lifeform
Watch it grow
Into what? You'll never know...

Some precious lifeform
Watch it grow

Into what? You'll never know... (3x)

Some precious lifeform
Watch it grow

Into what? You'll never know... (3x)

lion.

You can't do that, I'm King!!!
I don't think you'll like that.
King means everything.

(I don't think you'll like that)

You can't do that, I'm King!!!
I don't think you'll like that.
King means everything.

(I don't think you'll like that)

What are you bringing?
Please bring everything!
We all need your things
Even what you don't see...
Cause if you bring what you want
Then you won't have to flaunt.
But please bring everything.
Even private things...

(I don't think you'll like that)

You can't do that, I'm King!!!
I don't think you'll like that.
King means everything.

(I don't think you'll like that)

You can't do that, I'm King!!!
I don't think you'll like that.
King means everything.

my flow.

I know just what I want
Kindness and love up front
What I don't seem to know
Is if you like my flow

Do you like my flow?
Oh lord tell me so
Do you like my flow?

Cause if you really do
My love I'll give to you
So that you won't be blue
Livin' the life you choose.

Do you like my flow?
Oh please tell me so
Do you like my flow?

(bridge)

I know just what I want
Kindness and love up front
What I don't seem to know
Is if you like my flow

Do you like my flow?
Oh lord tell me so

Do you like my flow?

Cause if you really do
My love I'll give to you
So that you won't be blue
Livin' the life you choose.

Do you like my flow?
Oh please tell me so
Do you like my flow?
I know just what I want
Kindness and love up front.

nobody's home.

Nobody's home
Yeah!
I'm all alone
Yeah!
Nobody's home
Yeah!!!

I don't care, I don't care!

Where is the love at?
Where is my heart at?
Where is my heart at?

IT'S RIGHT HERE! (4x)

Nobody's home
Yeah!
I'm all alone
Yeah!
Nobody's home
Yeah!!!

I don't care, I don't care!

Where is my girlfriend?
Where is my mom at?
Where is my girl at?

SHE'S NOT HERE! (4x)

Nobody's home
Yeah!
I'm all alone
Yeah!

IT'S RIGHT HERE! (4x)

Where is my heart at?
Where is my heart at?
Where is my heart at?

IT'S RIGHT HERE! (4x)

one day hell.

One day hell,
one day hell for you.
One day hell,
one day hell for you.

Heaven must be love!
I haven't been this blasted.
OUTTA MY REALM!
I haven't been this blasted.
Outside of my realm!
I haven't been this blasted.
OUTTA MY REALM!
I haven't been this blasted.
Outside of my realm!
It's hell.

One day hell,
one day hell for you.
One day hell,
one day hell for me.

Heaven must be love!
I haven't been this blasted.
OUTTA MY REALM!
I haven't been this blasted.
Outside of my realm!
I haven't been this blasted.
OUTTA MY REALM!
I haven't been this blasted.
Outside of my realm!
It's hell.

One day hell.
One day hell.
One day hell.
One day hell?

pop off???

What's gonna pop off?
What's gonna pop off?
R&B, ROCK, JAZZ, OR HIP-HOP?
What's gonna pop off?
What's gonna pop off?
R&B, ROCK, JAZZ, OR HIP-HOP?
What's gonna pop off?
What's gonna pop off?
R&B, ROCK, JAZZ, OR HIP-HOP?
What's gonna pop off?
What's gonna pop off?
R&B, ROCK, JAZZ, OR HIP-HOP?

It's that time of night feelin' kinda buzzed
Goin' to the club off of that scudge
And a deuce-deuce of Bud
It be the Weiser
That be the shit that put me on fire
It sometimes makes me tired
But it's A.G. (all good)
And you know that we
Are gonna get down
And take away your frown
Cause it's that time of night
My life, my life, my life, my life
In the night time, YEAH!
My life, my life, my life, my life
In the night time, UH HUH!

(my life)

What's gonna pop off?
What's gonna pop off?
R&B, ROCK, JAZZ, OR HIP-HOP?
What's gonna pop off?
What's goona pop off?
R&B, ROCK, JAZZ, OR HIP-HOP?
What's gonna pop off?
What's gonna pop off?
R&B, ROCK, JAZZ, OR HIP-HOP?

(cont.)

It might be hip-hop if Greyboy is spinnin'
Or Rattyhead he'll be there chillin'
It won't be rock, it could be jazz
The ALLSTARS!
With the funky drummer Zack
Yeah the funky drummer Zack Najor
And you know that he is major
At hittin' the snares and the cymbals
And it's true that he'll pull strings
Strings, strings and diamond rings
And bring things that reign supreme
In the night time YEAH!
My life, my life, my life, my life
In the the night time UH HUH

(it's my life)

What's gonna pop off?
What's gonna pop off?
R&B, ROCK, JAZZ, OR HIP-HOP?
What's gonna pop off?
What's goona pop off?
R&B, ROCK, JAZZ, OR HIP-HOP?
What's gonna pop off?
What's goona pop off?
R&B, ROCK, JAZZ, OR HIP-HOP?
What's gonna pop off?
What's goona pop off?
YOUR SKIRT, YOUR PANTIES, YOUR BRA-TOP?

private things.

I don't know what it's coming to.
I don't know why you'd give my number.
Private things between me and you,
My business is not aired as public...

I don't know what it's coming to.
I don't know why you'd give my number.
Private things between me and you,
My business is not aired as public...

WHY MUST YOU TALK ON THE PHONE?
WHY MUST YOU TELL EVERYONE?

Why must you throw this old dog a bone?
Why must you give this old dog a home?

WHY MUST YOU TALK ON THE PHONE?
WHY MUST YOU TELL EVERYONE?

because you know that you want to
because you know that you want to
because you know that you want to
because you know that you want to
because you know that you want to
because you know that you want to

WHY MUST YOU TALK ON THE PHONE?
WHY MUST YOU TELL EVERYONE?

Why must you throw this old dog a bone?
Why must you give this old dog a home?

WHY MUST YOU TALK ON THE PHONE?
WHY MUST YOU TELL EVERYONE?

because you know that you want to
because you know that you want to
because you know that you want to
because you know that you want to
because you know that you want to
because you know that you want to

I don't know what it's coming to.
I don't know why you'd give my number.
Private things between me and you,
My business is not aired as public.

room of glass.

Behind, on the dark side of the room...
So close to the end, I dared not turn my back.
On you, cause you can't see them!
When you're in a room of glass.
I'm near the dark side of the room...

the room... (5x)

YEAH!

And I, I can't see them because...
It's so so clear, when you're in...
A room of glass.
When you're in a room made of glass.
WHEN YOU'RE IN A ROOM MADE OF GLASS!
MADE OF GLASS!
WHEN YOU'RE IN A ROOM.
Behind on the dark side of

the room... (5x)

YEAH!

I can't see them.
Because it's so so clear
When you're in a room of glass

of glass...(4x)

When you're in a room made of glass!
Living in a room made of glass!
When you're in a room MADE OF GLASS!!!
When you're in a room.

JIM SAID!!!
WHEN YOU'RE IN A ROOM MADE OF GLASS
WHEN YOU'RE IN A ROOM MADE OF GLASS
MADE OF GLASS
WHEN YOU'RE IN A ROOM...
MADE OF GLASS!!!

scream & holla.

Yeah it's crazy, these days and times...
2000 what?
People screamin' and hollerin' it's all about the dollar...
Material items, bling-bling...
Iced out medallions, luxury cars...

You scream and holla, it's all about the dolla!
Yes, you scream and holla, it's all about the dolla! (4x)

But it ain't! Without complaint, or graffiti paint,
You got to get yours, YO! Without restraint.
Cause livin' this life is a challenge,
And like I said you best to get some balance.
And you your skills.
Don't make no murder kills.
And keep it right like a Jedi Knight,
Only then will you acquire how to keep it tight.
Yes, keep it tight.

You scream and holla, it's all about the dolla!
Yes, you scream and holla, it's all about the dolla! (4x)

But it is! That's where I live!
I'm just tryin' to give!
Knowledge to all of you and yours,
And your kids!
Cause livin' this life is a challenge,
And like I said you best to get some balance.
And use your skills.
Don't make no murder kills.
And keep it right like a Jedi Knight,
Only then will you acquire how to keep it tight.
Yes, keep it tight.

You scream and holla, it's all about the dolla!
Yes, you scream and holla, it's all about the dolla! (4x)

There is no room for greed.
Only room for need.
Desire is what leads to misery.

sefuctress.

Can't stop thinkin' about you girl.
You been on my mind way too much.
(way too much)
You been on my mind way too much.
(way too much)

All that thinkin' gets mad frustrating sometimes.
A brother can't believe how he thinks of you...
No building, just straining.
A brother can't believe how he thinks of you...
Your love is draining.
A brother can't believe how he thinks of you...
My whole heart is raining.
I'm not even complaining.

How he...

Just simply stating that you ain't really down for Reeves
Ya betta ask Jeeves
Always somethin' up my sleeves, seductress
You just wanna get high and fuck this
Till you come hard like an actress
While you're layin' on your back
On my mattress?
Givin' me God knows what
I can match this
So get it in gear
Listen up clear
Come over here

And... suck this, feel this, love this, freak this, sex this, impress this, kiss this, hold this, hug this, sex this, caress this, maintain this, claim this, explain this, exchange this, rearrange this, create this, make this, hug this, kiss this, love this, fuck this.

You love me you say this.
But I cannot feel it.
You been on my mind way too much.
(way too much)
You been on my mind way too much.
(way too much)

It's mad frustrating sometimes... way too much, thinking about you 24/7 girl goodnight sweet dreams.

she's so sweet.

Well I, was going to the air
THE AEROPUERTO!
Yes! One day. Yes! One day.

Well I, was going to the Lon-the-London town
To see my girl, see my babe!

She's so sweet, like a peach...
She's so sweet, strawberries...

Well I, got on the plane
I sat, I sat in my seat
Had a drink, had twelve drinks
And then twelve hours later
I, was greeted by the sweetest girl
DONA!

She's so sweet, like a peach...
She's so sweet, strawberries...

Well, I was going to the Van-Vancouver town
To see my girl, see my babe!

She's so sweet, like a peach...
She's so sweet, strawberries...

(cont.)

Well I, got on the plane
I sat, I sat in my seat
Had a drink, had six drinks
And then six hours later
I, was greeted by the sweetest girl
TATIANA!

She's so sweet, like a peach...
STRAWBERRY...

Well, I was going to the Port-Portland town
To see my girl, see my babe!

She's so sweet, like a peach...
She's so sweet, strawberries...

Well I, got on the plane
I sat, I sat in my seat
Had a drink, had four drinks
And then four hours later
I, was greeted by the sweetest girl
MARISSA!

She's so sweet, like a peach...
STRAWBERRY...

SHE'S SO SWEET! (4x)

shit don't matter in SD.

Shit don't matter in SD.

(Lampin' out hard...)

We be cold kickin' back in SD.
Shit don't matter in SD.
Yo, it's laid back son!
Moon and stars. 1904 to the world.
(619) (858) (760) the MECCA!
PQ. Golden Hills!

(That's where I dwell... with the golden kids.)

Mission Beach. PB. Chula Vista.
Jungle beats. The Beach.
Fat ass hip-hop beats.
Bongos, palm trees, sunlight.
Mad Mayans! Mad Mayans? Mad Mayans? MAD MAYANS!
AZTECS, PADRES, CHARGERS, LA RAZA!

I eat some Papayans.
And then I get the fuckin' mango with my girl.
Rock the world!
And then go give her a pearl.
Necklace cause I'm gonna have to wreck this...
And then I eat the mango on a sweet bed of rice.
The Thai spice sounds so nice.
I like it like that and I won't say it twice.
What's gonna pop off every night?
Staying sane is what I'm gonna do...
When I'm in the MECCA with the MMC crew.
(La Jolla. Point Loma.)
Cause you know that's where I dwell.

(Blacks Beach. Ho Chi Minh trail.)

(cont.)

So all you silly suckas can just go to hell.
If you don't like that.
Cause you know I'm FAT!
And you know the label was FAT that rocked that!

(Carlsbad. Oceanside. Del Mar.)

From tenth street caffeinated designs.
You know I like that shit cause you know my shit shines!
Like the sun that dances on the water.
What'd you say? I ain't the Bantha fodder!

(Come along young padawan and learn about SD.)

I came like that! What?

(OB. Palm trees. Oceans. Mad chronic.)

I came like this, keep it crisp. Hit don't miss.
Cause it must be crisp.

(Do you want to be frozen in solid carbonite?)

Because... Shit don't matter in SD.
It just don't matter in SD.
Blazin', Blazin', Blazin'
Blazin' trails of evil in SD.

Laid back blazin' trees in SD.
You can't beat the weather in SD.
Nothing's better than the weather in SD.

shoot the moon.

You wish it would all end
Everything that you begin
You wish it would begin
All good things come to an end

But you got to just shoot the moon
Yeah you got to, you got to just shoot moon
Yeah just shoot the moon yeah you're going to
You've got to just shoot the moon

Don't let minor setbacks get you down
You better do your best to win the crown
Don't let minor setbacks get you down
You gotta turn that frown right upside down

And you will, just shoot the moon
Yeah you got to, you got to just shoot moon
Yeah just shoot the moon yeah you're going to
You've got to just shoot the moon

Do your best, stay positive
Only then will you really live
Minor setbacks, can't hold you down
You better show them all you hold the sound

And then you'll shoot the moon
Yeah you got to, you got to just shoot moon
Yeah just shoot the moon yeah you're going to
You've got to just shoot the moon

slinky.

It's like a slinky, it must retract.
You're on this surface, we can't reflect.

Everything you do and see,
Is on their level...
Come into the underground,
You know it's mellow...

You've got to find it!
Inside of you.
And only then,
Will you know what to do.
Finding a balance is a challenge.
And when you get it, you will extend...

What you see, and how they act,
Ain't always facts...
Take just what's inside your own heart,
To find exacts...

You feel the truth inside yourself,
And you know that is worth the world...
It's like a slinky, it must retract.
You're on this surface, we can't reflect.

Everything you do and see
Is on their level...
Come into the underground
You know it's mellow.

social scene.

You must feel sorry in the social scene
Everything matters in the social scene
If we cannot be what we see
We can only try to plot, devise, realize!

That you're not the same in the social scene
You're not the same social scene
That you're not the same in the social scene
People are sorry for their own self being
They doubt to try to stop the clinging
Shopping for an old beat up TV

And you are sorry... you are sorry
And you ask me?

Why I'm not the same in the social scene?
Why I'm not the same social scene?
Why I'm not the same in the social scene?
Why I'm not the same in the social scene?
Why I'm not the same social scene?
Why I'm not the same in the social scene?

You must feel sorry in the social scene
Everything matters in the social scene
If we cannot be what we see
We can only try to plot, devise, realize!

That you're not the same in the social scene
You're not the same social scene

THE SOCIAL SCENE.

souperman.

What is goin' on
I been waitin' for so long
And you had said
You'd be over in the end
I'll never go away
I'll just wait and stay
Who do I think I am?
Some kind of souperman?

I heard it all before
most people just want more.
I heard it all before
most people just want more.

Who do I think I am?
Some kind of souperman?
Who do I think I am?
Some kind of souperman?

What is goin' on
I been waitin' for so long
And you had said
You'd be leavin' in the end

I'll never go away
I'll just wait and stay
Who do I think I am?
Some kind of souperman?

stayin' sane.

Stayin' sane
Livin' in uncertainty
I'm lookin' around
Fuckin' feelin'
Anxiety
Right or wrong
You decide
Insanity is what it provides
You cannot see it, it's so bright
Unless you're standing in front of the light...
There was a wind
A wind that smelled like death
And you can't
You can't control your breath
I don't know what you want from me
But take what you can
Take what you need
I don't know what you want from me
But take what you can
Take what you need
Take what you need, what you need
Take what you need.

sunny's happy song.

Don't let what you think
Get in the way of what you believe
Just be true and then you will be happy
You'll be happy
Sunny is the middle name of my girlie
My girlie
This is Sunny's happy song oh can't you see
Can't you see

That this is Sunny's happy song
Sunny's happy song
That this is Sunny's happy song
Sunny's happy song yeah!
That this is Sunny's happy song
This is a sunny happy song!

If you really think you can
Then you will, you will succeed
Just like breathing
Some things are just meant to be
Meant to be
Use your mind, you know you can do anything
Anything
Do everything

Cause this is Sunny's happy song
Sunny's happy song
Cause this is Sunny's happy song yeah!
Sunny's happy song
This is a sunny happy song!

the truth is mine.

Had you here, my love
Now you're gone my loss
Maybe I, I didn't know
How to be in love

(no, not with you)

The truth is mine, the choice yours
The truth is mine, the choice yours
The truth is mine, the choice yours
The truth is mine, the choice yours

Now I'm so lonely
I can't fake happy
So I must be free
Let you go party

(yeah, yes you know you will)

The truth is mine, the choice yours
The truth is mine, the choice yours
The truth is mine, the choice yours
The truth is mine, the choice yours

Now you'll be happy
And I'll be misery
'Til I find that thing
Then I'll be IRIE... yeah

The truth is mine, the choice yours
The truth is mine, the choice yours
The truth is mine, the choice yours
The truth is mine, the choice yours

Had you here, my love
Now you're gone my loss
Maybe I, I didn't know
How to be in love

(no, not with you)

The truth is mine, the choice yours
The truth is mine, the choice yours
The truth is mine, the choice yours
The truth is mine, the choice yours

time is now.

Time is now
Scream out loud
Time is now

So scream out loud (2x)

I know you know
So you know I know
Go with the flow
And win the show
You think it's cool
Oh now it's cool
To be a fool
Is Fonzie cool!
To be a fool
Is Fonzie cool?

Time is now
Scream out loud
Time is now

So scream out loud (2x)

We all could know
We all should know
That we're the same
Just different coverings
We all need things
All girls need rings
We all should sing
And do our thing!
We all need things
So come on sing!

Time is now
Scream out loud
Time is now

So scream out loud (2x)

what's it really worth?

You tip the bong.
Now you spilling bong wahtah!
You drink vodka.
Now you feel ya brain splattah!
You know what life can show you...
You've got to really know...
Live righteous, and live true yah!
Like Rasta straight from birth...
You tip the bong
Now you spilling bong wahtah!
You drink vodka
Now you feel ya brain splattah!

What's it really worth?
What's it really worth?
What's it really worth?
What's it really worth?

You tip the bong.
Now you spilling bong wahtah!
You drink vodka.
Now you feel ya brain splattah!
You know what life can show you...
You've got to really know...
Live righteous, and live true yah!
Like a Rasta straight from Earth...
You tip the bong.
Now you spilling bong wahtah!
You drink vodka.
Now you feel ya brain splattah!

What's it really worth?
What's it really worth?
What's it really worth?
What's it really worth?

you can love.

You can love, you can love, you can love, you can love.
Did you know that you could?
Did you know that you could?
You can love, you can love, you can love, you can love.
Did you know that you could?
Did you know that you could?

Things fall down, things fall down, things fall down, things fall down.
But you knew that they would.
And you knew that they could.
Things fall down, things fall down, and things break, and things break.
But you knew that they would.
And you knew that they would.
And things break, yes things break, and things break, and things break.
And you knew that they would.
Cause you knew that they would.

You can love, you can love, you can love, you can love.
Did you know that you could?
Did you know that you could?
Did you know that you could?
Did you know that you could?

You can love, you can love, you can love, you can love.
Did you know that you could?
Did you know that you would?
Did you know that you would?
Did you know that you would?
Did you know that you would?
Did you know that you would?

you come up.

You come up...
And
You come down...
You, get high and you stumble around, you...

You come up...
And
You come down...
You, get drunk and you fumble around, you...

Just to get back to the place where you're from!
Never forgetting just who's number one!
Even when things seem to get kinda rough!
Never forgetting just who's hella tough!

You come up and you come down
You get cream and you live dreams
You come up and you come down
You get cream and you live dreams, you...

(bridge)

You come up.
And
You come down.
You, get high and you stumble around, you...
You come up.
And
You come down.
You, get drunk and you fumble around, you...

Just to get back to the place where you're from!
Never forgetting that you're number one!
Even when things seem to get kinda rough!
Never forgetting that you're so hella tough!

You come up and you come down...
You.

LISTS

death or responsibility.

1. GRADUATE.

2. DEATH MASK.

3. A BOY AND HIS DOG.

4. SLIPPIN' MICKEY.

5. DEATH OR RESPONSIBILITY.

Pencil Ones.

1. GO KISS A DUCK.

2. BEARS AND SQUIRRELS.

3. CIRCLE OF LIFE.

4. I'M STILL SUING.

5. RETURN THE MONEY.

6. TECHNO BIRD.

7. PIERCED LOVE.

8. OODLES OF NOODLES.

9. BODEGA BIRD GANG.

10. AM I GOING TO DIE?

11. ROUND STONES.

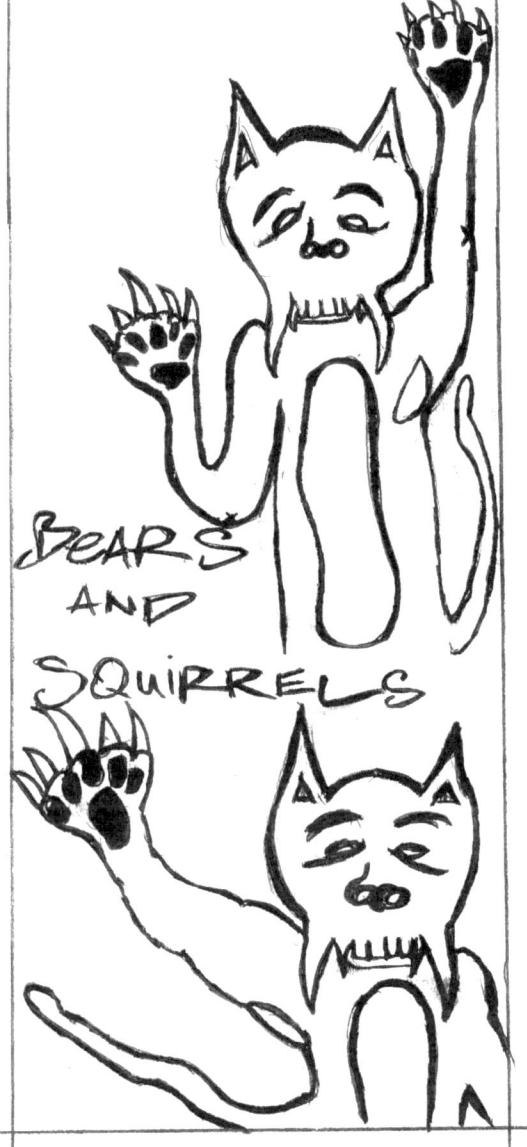

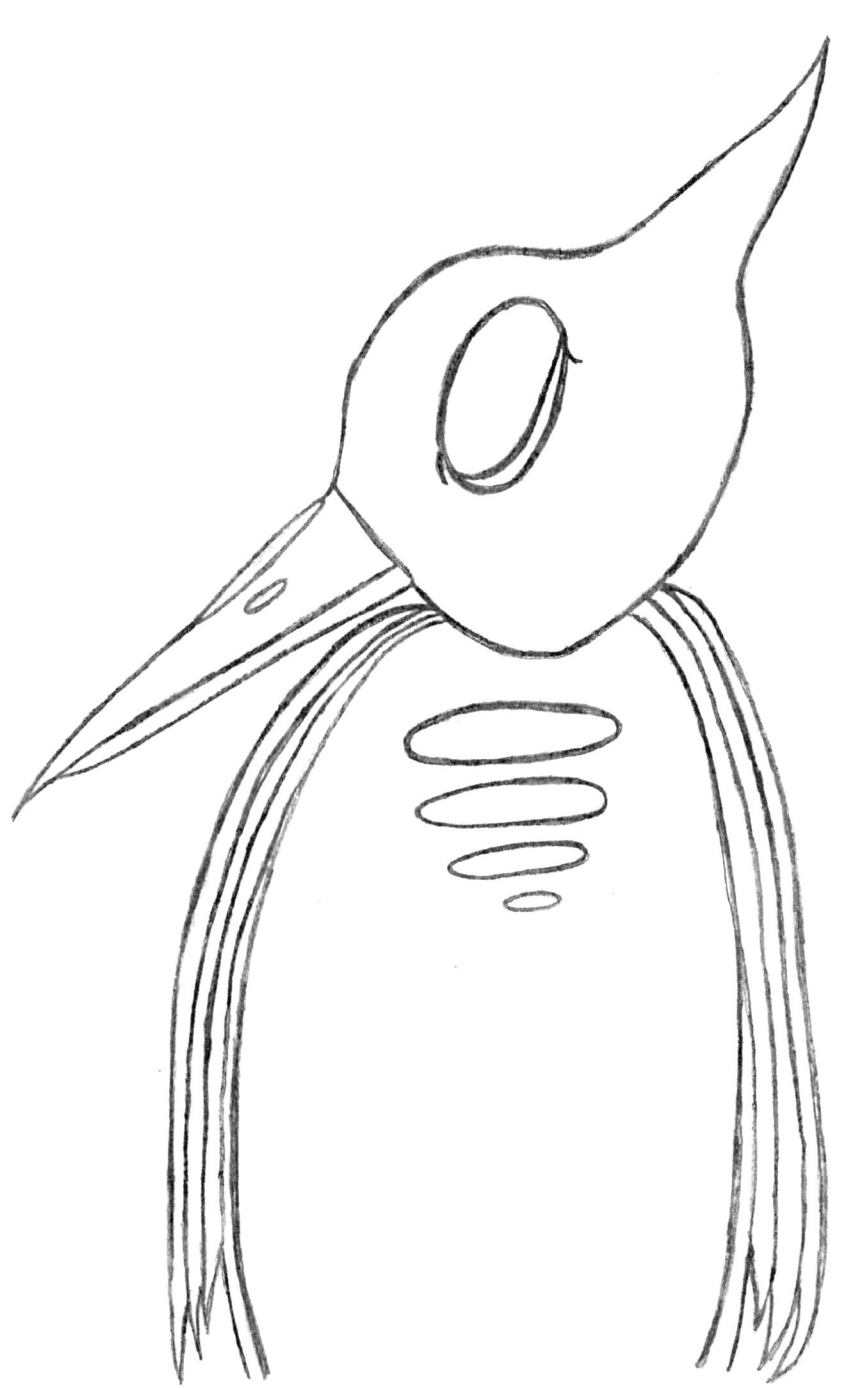

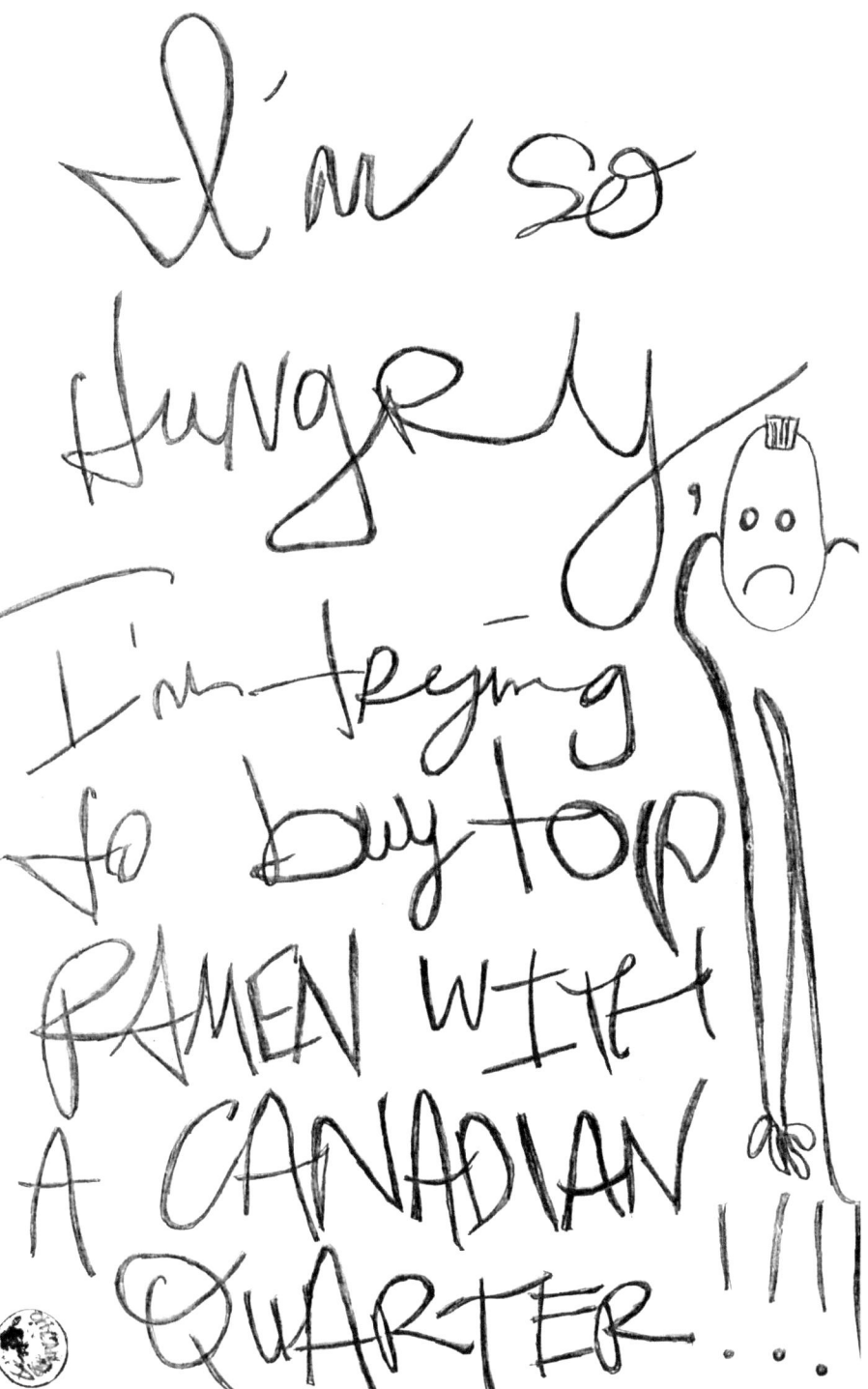

quotes.

"the essential component of a yo-yo is the string. with all of the ups and downs, it is important to keep the string tight."

"there is no room for awkwardness, there is only room for life."

"threats only make the rebel more rebellious."

"who says anything, and after they say it, does it really mean what they said?"

"without love you are hurt... with love you are hurt."

"everyone is in a hole. the thing to do is to try to make your hole a little less deep."

"the more creative I become, the more I realize that art and the concept of creation can affect more in the idea state."

"for me it is not so much the skills of the artist... it is the idea, the creative original thought... genuine concepts rule."

"with observation, and many, many grueling hours of study I've come up with a theory: if one is one dimensional, then one is no one."

"no soldier is stronger than love, and I will second that notion. some are stronger than pride, those are the soldiers that are willing to die."

"time is not a handcuff. time is a gun. you risk it all in the name of freedom."

the baggie series.

1. REAL BLOOD.

2. TEAR.

3. I. N. I = REAL PERSON.

4. GRIPFACE.

5. CAT-EYE SHOULDER GUYS.

6. BUMPFACE.

7. MATCHSTICKFACE.

the black nail project.

1. BLACK PINKY.

2. BANQUET BEER.

3. COMI.

4. WATCH VAGINA.

5. BELT VAGINA.

6. BACK TO LONDON.

7. AS I AM.

8. UMBRELLA SMOKE.

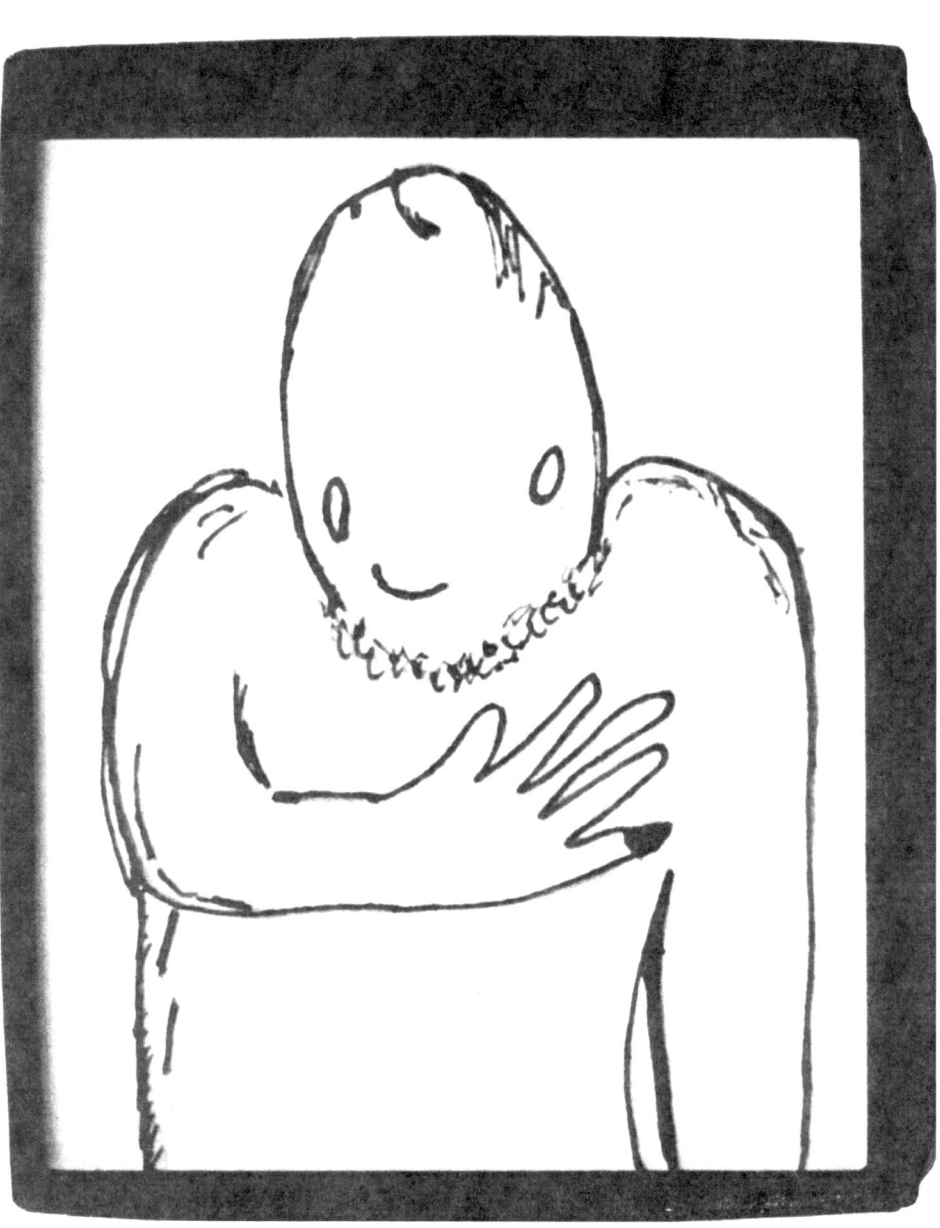

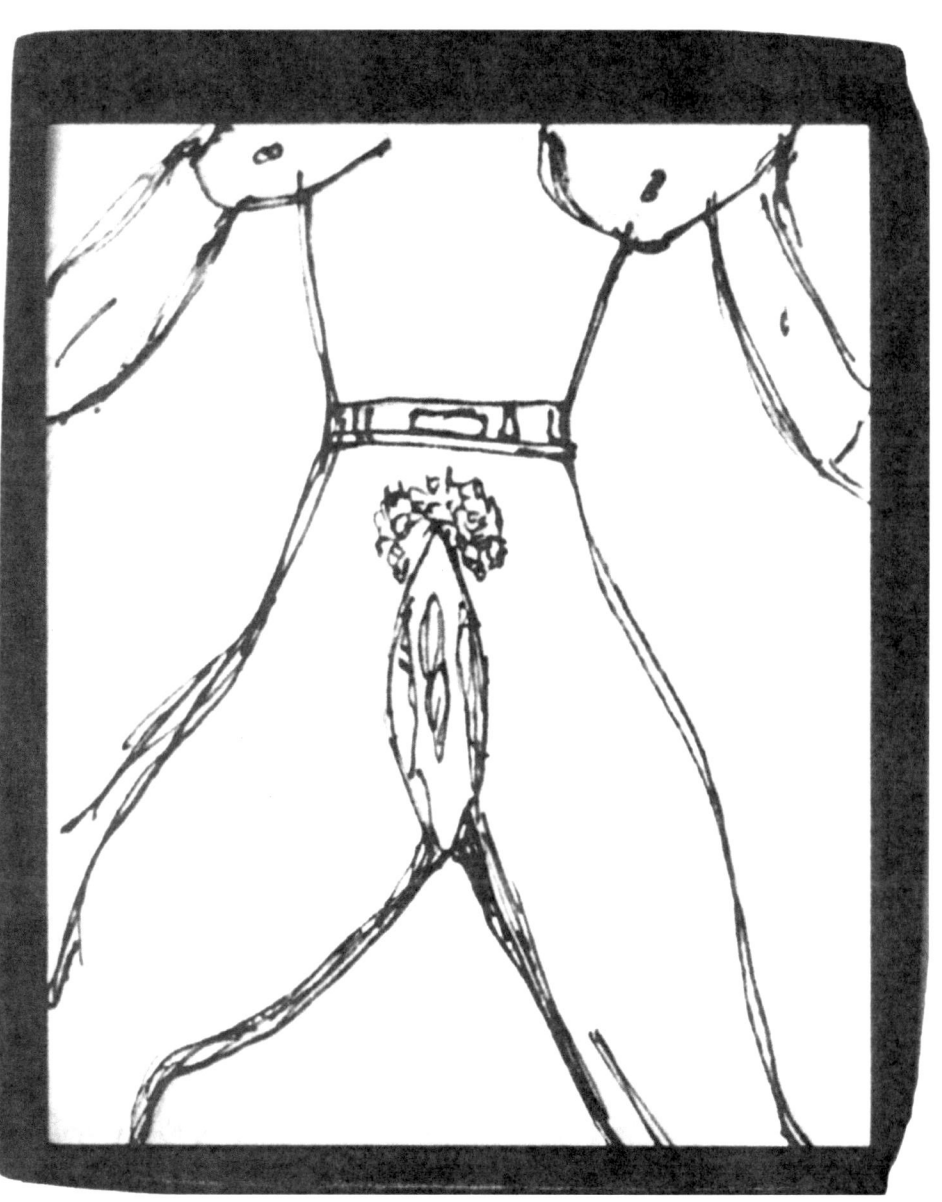

SHORTS

3 wishes.

If I had three wishes...
My first wish would be...
My first wish would be able to see through my eyelids.
I would like to see all of the activity.
I would like to see what happens around me when my eyes are closed.
I think many people would like to have that kind of power.
To see what lurks in the darkest of hours.
Especially the hours spent stuck on the train or in the rain during heavy showers.
Though, surprisingly, I am starting to enjoy the train, and the rain.
And that is precisely the reason why I would like to be able to see through my eyelids.
Imagine closing your eyes in the rain and still being able to see!

It seems weird to call *the subway, the train.*
However I like to call the subway, the train.
Hell, I like to call the subway "THE IRON WORM."
I heard it called *The Iron Worm* in the melting pot mix or on the street somewhere.
In some unruly cipher. In some magical place.
In some magical place with a destination unaware.
A place with a bunch of heads talking a bunch of shit.
I don't know who first called the subway the train.
I don't know who first called the subway the iron worm.
But somehow it makes the subway seem bigger.
Somehow it makes it seem like every ride that I take on the train is an adventure.
It makes it seem as if I am departing from reality.
It makes it feel like as if I am embarking onto lands never before traveled.
That's why. That is exactly why I guess I will be riding the subway, train, or the iron worm, as I like to call it, for the rest of my life even if my second wish comes true.
When I was growing up the train was called the "*choo choo*" and the "*choo choo*" was above ground.
The locomotive meant a lot. The locomotive meant freedom, it meant America.
The locomotive meant being able to travel.
The locomotive meant that an individual could travel state to state and do it in a relatively short amount of time.

That brings us to my second wish.
This second wish deals directly with travel.
Specifically with traveling vast distances in a short amount of time.
My second wish would be to be able to teleport.
Not necessarily to travel through time, but to be able to go anywhere you would like; to go with pure thought. Meaning, you think it, you live it.

Speaking of thinking it and living it... that brings us to my third wish.
I guess that means that;
My third wish would be to be myself!
I think it and I live it.

death, funny papers, and vapors.

Death, funny papers, and vapors. In this day and age you must, and I strongly emphasize the word must, have a healthy sense of humor. Sure, I know people grow up in different places, have different cultures, and are raised differently. However, even if you have gone through some serious trials and/or tribulations, I believe that to get past those things, an individual needs to be able to look back at whatever trial or tribulation they went through and laugh at it, or at least laugh with it.

The way I see it is simple... life can suck, but no matter what, whoever is born, and I don't care who it is, they are privileged to have the opportunity to laugh, fight, cry, and love. That means that they are lucky to be alive. Come on just look at it. If they were never born they would never know shit! There is no way that they would know the extremes of life. They would never know how joyous or how sickening life can be. They would never ever ever ever know the crazy, inane, insane circumstances that the human animal can get into! With all the wrong in the world, sometimes laughing at it just seems right.

the magical mini-bar bottle of jameson.

DID THEY?
Did they? Did they? Did they even make a mini-sized bottle of Jameson Whiskey? The very same whiskey that John Jameson had once fought an octopus for?
Do they make a small version?
I wonder if they really do?

It just so happens that they do!
And the first one that I ever had was magnificent!!!
Yeah it was and that experience was, plus still is, way beyond comprehension. With that said, I mean that the average would not understand and they might get scared; additionally if they hear the rest of the story then; F-U-C-K ! ! !

The average will not understand and they might get scared.
Might as well just subtract the *might get scared* part.
They will get scared, they might be scared enough to nix the rest of this story!
But I do not want that to happen, this is not a horror story.
Shit, this shit not even a sex crazy maniacal sexual thriller.
This is simply the story of a magical mini bottle of whiskey.

Yes, I drink beer. Who doesn't? I haven't met anyone who doesn't drink beer in a very long time. Yeah it has definitely been quite a while since I met an individual who does not drink beer. So yes, do you enjoy beverages? I assume that you do, but who wants to make an ass out of "u" and "me"? Not me, not anybody. You know that you like beer! If you didn't then you probably would not be reading this story.
And that is how it all starts. (Fade in music "Sober" by Tool)

(Open zoomed in on the mini-fridge)

(cont.)

So I am just a simple businessman (accountant) on a business trip that is geared to make all of the numbers add up. I am just a guy on a short business trip to make sure that all of the numbers align, so that we can make this business merger a success. Everything is already in preparation and prepared for success. That means to say, that everything is sync'd up, the money is in place, the words have been exchanged, everybody is on the same page, so there should be minimal confusion! I mean that everybody is on the up & up, everyone is square. So square or not? I still am obligated to meet up with them 24 hours from now, but at least I get to go to the hotel lobby bar, check into my hotel room and settle in for the night before the big meeting. Having already experienced such a long tedious travel day with anything and everything going wrong; a couple of beers, a few shots and then the mini-bar are well deserved. And I will gladly share the spoils of my mini bar with one of these sexy office troglodykes; gotta love the lobby bar!
Damn! She wouldn't roll, why wouldn't that sexy troglodyke roll back to my room with me? Oh well, hopefully I have a little bottle of Jameson waiting for me back at the room! Wait a minute do they even make a mini bottle of Jameson?
I know they make Absolute, Jack Daniels, Johnnie Walker, VSOP, Belvedere, Grey Goose, Seagrams, Smirnoff, Ricard, Disaronno, Bailey's and Jagermeister bottles that size, but do they make Jameson in that size?

So as the story continues... no mini-bottle of Jameson.
What really happened? Was there really no mini-bottle of Jameson? I thought that I had already saw it! I could practically taste it! So if it's only Absolute, Jack Daniels, Johnnie Walker, VSOP. Belvedere, Grey Goose, Seagrams, Smirnoff, Ricard, Disaronno, Bailey's, and Jagermeister that make those mini-bottles, then that absolutely (by any human being's standard) means that I have to start a quest to find and consume this mini-bottle of Jameson.
Yes a quest! A quest until this magical mini-bottle of Jameson is mine!!!
MUAHHHAHHHHHAHHHHAHHHHAA!!!
Of course the night is still young. It's only 11:30...

me bad?

      Why? Why can't I write something? Something that people actually want to read. Anything, a short story, a novel, a book, a novella, fuck! I don't care, I don't even know what a fucking novella is. All I know is that I just need to get this off of my chest.
      I wake up, crusty as hell from a night of debauchery and all out animalism. Where am I? Soho, Midtown, or the Lower East Side? I'm just guessing cause those are the places that I frequent. It sucks waking up with this taste in your mouth. Although, I did have fun slaying dragons and pillaging whores. I can't stand waking to this taste. My mouth tastes like Miles pissed and shit in it. My mouth tastes like I licked the bottom of his litter box, and it is just as dry. If you didn't figure it out by now, Miles is my cat. Or should I say our cat?
      I lie facedown on someone else's dirty pillow and makeshift bed of sofa cushions of which I could only use the small ones due to the other dude already passed out on the couch. I was wrong I'm not in Soho, Midtown, or the Lower East Side; I'm in Chinatown. I'm in the area where Laurence Fishburne and Christopher Walken had an all out war with Chinese drug lords in "The King of New York" and I need to get out. Lucky? Talk about lucky, I passed out, I mean passed out on Candi's floor. Candi is my friend's girlfriend. She smells like one of my ex-girlfriends. Gucci Rush; I could smell that perfume anywhere, cause it is French, and so was my ex-girlfriend. I'll never forget that perfume because it is one of the only brands of perfume that I actually ever purchased. I bought it when I had good credit and a brand new card from a prominent department store in Southern California. It is so memorable because I had gotten it thirteen hours before. I also had a detailed conversation with the older hot perfume girl about my plans. When I say plans I mean what I was going to do with the perfume. The saleswomen was so excited when she found out that I was going to fly to the South of France and present it to my fiancé. She was only my girlfriend but the story sounded way more romantic when I said that we were getting married.
      Anyway, let us get back to Candi. I wanted her, but that would not have been kosher with my girlfriend or bueno with her boyfriend. I use kosher in my girlfriend's case because she is Jewish, and I use bueno because he is latino. Come to think of it, I believe Candi is Jewish too. What is it with me and Jewish women? I don't know, who cares, this isn't about them. This is about me. Plus it doesn't hurt that she is named after my drug of choice. It just makes her that much more desirable, like to the power of ten. After all, Candi does make you feel dandy. I try to leave. But my body doesn't respond. I am beyond the point of hung over. I need a drink. I am hot, dry, wet, cold and bitter all at the same time. It is forty-three past high noon and I already hear voices in the loft. Oh, I didn't tell you? Candi lives in a loft. A loft full of artists, skaters, filmmakers, photographers, and all out creative people. I feel lucky to be there. I need to be around these types of people, so that I can hone my craft. What is my craft? I'd say anything that doesn't require heavy lifting. I'm done with that. Spontaneity is my thing. I think it and I do it. Sometimes I don't even think, I just do.
      I need to get out of this place. I stand up. Luckily I passed out with my jacket and sneakers on, this way nothing will be left behind. I can't move correctly, my body needs rest. It wants me to keep lying down. It wants me to give it just one more hour of rest, but my mind says something completely different. My mind and ears are listening. Sirens, voices, people are already in it going, moving, swimming

(cont.)

through the urban abyss of life that happens in the big city. My body never wants to join them but my mind does. It tells me I'm too smart to be lazy, it says join the race, you can win. Unfortunately I believe it. So I go. I get up and work my way to the door. I try to open it but I fail. You would think I was in a maximum security prison. There is this crazy lock on the door. A huge arm bar lock and I don't know how to open it. I try. I am weak. I try again and I can't unlock it. This is embarrassing because I am being watched. Candi's roommate is watching me fumble with the door. Her name is Lori and she is fighting the urge of laughing at me because I cannot open the door. She is hot, like a young Goldie Hawn with the hair, smile, and body to play Goldie in a movie. This place is as secure as Fort Knox. It has some kind of crazy arm lock that I am too drunk, or too dumb, to open. She helps me. I need a drink. She gets the lock undone and I thank her and proceed to stumble down the dirty, old, decrepit stairs of the loft building down to the street. I end up in a way too bright, way too busy world.

  Left or right? Does it matter? This is my next critical choice. There is no way to prognosticate my next move. I can't keep living like this. Couch to couch, floor to floor with delusions of grandeur. Between all of the different cities and different faces I'm just a shell of myself, riddled with pieces of every individual whose path I have crossed. But that doesn't matter. What matters now is left or right? Could it be a wrong move? A twist or turn into a dark scary corner? I need to make this decision. One way could be the path that needs to be taken, and the other could lead to an ultimate demise. I choose left. Should I have gone right? It doesn't matter now, I have already made my decision and there is no turning back. Left. Left is as good of a choice as any. It points deeper into Chinatown towards Soho, and that is the way I need to go. In a flash, I decide I'm getting a hot sake and a large Kirin to keep me going. Maybe I'll get that Vietnamese beef noodle soup that I had wanted the night before. Yeah, that's it, I'll find a nice rice noodle bowl place with a liquor license and a hot waitress to boot.

  I'm walking left across Canal Street, dodging septic puddles and speeding automobiles. Whoa, I've never seen this. An outdoor, indoor soccer field imbedded in the heart of the city. It breathes with Asian manchildren who just want to make a goal. There are about two or three white guys in the mix too. One of whom has only one arm. I guess that is better for soccer since you can't touch the ball with your hands unless you're the goalie anyway. I stop and watch. I stand there for ten minutes and not one goal is scored. Boring. I haven't played soccer since 7th grade physical education, and don't plan to ever again. It's not that I don't like soccer, it's just that I guess now that I am older I don't have as much patience for organized sports. I am more into organized crime.

  I need a drink. I need to keep moving plus there is this fat old guy smoking a stinking ass cigar and I'm downwind. If I inhale one more whiff of his stogie I'm sure I'll hurl. An epic hurl, probably pure alcohol seeing as how that's all that I put in my system last night. I eventually get across the street and deeper into Chinatown. People are everywhere selling this and buying that; it is a veritable stew of people clawing and practically walking on top of each other. The monkeys, angels, and devils inhabiting my neck, shoulders, and back are nothing compared to my current home life situation; so I guess I don't mind the people on top of people in these filthy streets.

(cont.)

Pho Hoa and a sake. Yeah that's it. That is what I need, yeah and that ice cold brew, any beer will do domestic or import. These things will give me the energy and the nefarious, gregarious, mind state to keep going. They will also provide me with an outlook not to do anything too crazy. I also could use some aspirin. A whole bottle of Bayer to make my blood thinner, and reduce my risk of a heart attack, or a stroke. I could use a couple of Advil PM gel tabs for the anesthetic and tranquilizing effects. The pharmaceutical industry consists of a bunch of pirates. Legalized drug dealers who are getting richer by the second with no regard to the people out of their tax brackets. And the insurance companies that get paid twice. Fuck, all insurance companies do is get paid. Well, I guess there are the few who actually want people to feel better, they call that palliative care. Drugging people so that they don't feel pain while they die. I'm pretty sure they do not want to cure anybody, because then they would be out of a job.

Later for that, I need food, I need nourishment. Mott Street. Oh, this on the edge of Soho and Chinatown, and I think there is a spot near here where I can get what I need. As I continue down the right side of Mott Street, I am scanning left to right. There is an old Chinese restaurant sign above this place that looks as if it is out of business. As I get closer I see some letters on the window that say R-I-C-E and a couple of people eating in this narrow dining room. So I enter. Thinking I am going to be greeted by some Confucius type waiter, I am greeted by the complete opposite. An ultra styled out non-Asian hipster girl with a nice rack. I get excited, and smoothly tell her what I want and need.

"Give me a bowl of Pho and a hot sake with a cold beer." I say without skipping a beat. She smiles and says, "Just one second I'll be right with you. You can have a seat over there. Did you say you wanted beef noodle soup?"

I say, "Yeah, PHO HOA!" and scuffle over to where she had instructed me to sit. Next thing I know there is a large hot sake and a cold beer in front of me and I am jubilated.

She just threw them down without spilling a drop and was on her way back to the kitchen when I blurted out, "Do you mind pouring me the first one? Just the first one?"

She comes back and does exactly what I asked saying, "I'm the same way when it comes to sake."

I say, "Thank you. Thank you," and zone out on her fine ass as she returned to the kitchen.

Less than a minute later I receive my bowl of PHO and it's like AW OH UM!!! I mean the heavens crossed the Earth and the sky opened up. I didn't know whether to thank the waitress with money or congratulate her with a job well done. However, I know that my old school homie, Steve Tran from Redding, California who introduced me to Vietnamese noodle soup, would have done both.

Next thing I know I need more meat. I'm a carnivore. I like flesh. The flesh of the young and old, particularly the good looking. Women young and old, I would eat them. I would eat them up like a Little Debbie, Hostess, or Drake's snack cake. I would not digest them just nibble and lick in a loving, caring way. I cannot forget to mention Tastykakes. I think they are made in Philadelphia, Pennsylvania. Peanut butter candy cakes; those are my favorite. I've told this to girls and women before. I want

(cont.)

to eat them all up like a snack cake. Some hits some misses. You'd be surprised to learn that some women are always waiting for someone to talk to them like that. Hard and fast.

Anyhow, let us get back to my soup. A nice array of beef, noodles, vegetables and broth, all of which I'm salivating for. Clear rice noodles, bean sprouts, hot peppers, cilantro, onions, beef, and beef broth. Did I say I was a carnivore? The only stuff I need to add is mint leaves, soy sauce, and sriracha. Maybe a little plum sauce for sweetness. Sriracha is the sauce, the hot sauce. And this time I might have gone overboard with it. You have probably seen it before, a big red bottle with a rooster on it with a green top. Most call it rooster sauce. Anyway, I love it and will not eat PHO HOA without it.

It is time for beer. This is one of the most important parts of my day. The beer, that is. When I first see it I'm ready. First a little sip, then a straight up gulp, and then a pound. But only after the first shot of sake. I need more meat. I know I need more solid food in my system. All of this liquid might not work with the way that I'm feeling. So I order some beef jerky. No, not like the kind you get at a Wawa, Seven Eleven, or a Circle K. This shit is premium USDA choice steak cut into small sliced slivers and seasoned to perfection. Ready to eat with chopsticks. Yeah now you're talking.

After a couple of more shots of sake, I'm feeling back to normal; except one thing. I either need to shit or vomit. I opt for the shit. The bathroom is small. Small but clean, and I am thankful for the cleanliness. I should have brought something to read. I don't think this thing will end real soon. That one guy who said, "Reading and writing is like a never ending homework assignment," was right. It is like a homework assignment, but no one is going to grade it, unless you have a publisher or you're reading orally. Let us get back to my shit. Bowel movement, poop, crap, whatever you want to call it, I was done. It had come out pretty smooth, even under these circumstances. It might have stunk, however I am the first to admit that I think mine smells kind of good. It smells better when you're not drunk, I guess it has something to do with the vital organ called the liver. It was a job well done and I was extremely proud of myself for doing a number two in a public bathroom. With that out of the way...

I'm back at the table and ready to pay the bill and get the fuck out. I sit and observe the others in an attempt to not be impatient. There are a couple of girls who just got their appetizer. An older couple is in the heart of their meal. And there is one man sitting alone ready to pay his bill. That man is I. The girls are kind of cute and fun to look at, but I need to leave.

Dry. Drier than dry, drier than a million deserts, drier than a billion deserts, drier than a trillion deserts with a hot wind, hotter than your girl's ass, hotter than your girl's blow drier, hotter than your girl's curling iron. That is where I am. That is how I feel when I wake from a dream like this. Sometimes I dream so hard that I am literally tired when I wake up. Like I had no sleep at all, no rest for the wicked. There I am. Surrounded. Three hundred and sixty degrees by desert, cacti, caverns, and carved spires brightly, brilliantly adobe colored earth orange-red, with a little burnt sienna. There are a plethora of plateaus painted by millions of years of lava, volcanoes, water, wind, fire, and any other geological changes that you or anyone could think of. Where am I? Am I in some dinosaur Jurassic age? That is what it looks like, but it feels like I

(cont.)

am in the middle of a Southern California apartment complex. I think that is where I am. I am not alone. This dream is a trip. There are three other people around and I have no idea who they are. We are not accomplishing anything. We are just kind of floating in this Utah-esque, Arizona deserty apartment complex in Southern California. I need to get out of this dream and back to the city. Although, the scenery here is quite pleasant, it is a far cry from the high rises and sounds of the city, but I like it; maybe there is something to accomplish here. But what could it be? What could possibly be accomplished in this barren desolate area? What am I supposed to do in this large, dry, ill-lucid region that is entirely devoid of life? The others here are faceless silhouettes of humans that are definitely trapped here. I do not want to be trapped here... so I must wake up. Could this be hell? Could this be heaven? I'm not ready for either of those so I force myself to wake up. The key is to stay sane in this unforgiving, cold, cold world. Sometimes we cannot be what we see and this frustrates us. I don't care who you are, this is a frustrating concept for all.

Suddenly I'm on Mott Street again walking out of Soho. Somehow I'm heading downtown towards the Brooklyn Bridge and the Supreme Court. Mott, almost cool enough or should I say almost too cool. With all of the specialty stores and fancy boutiques selling Couture, how could anyone be cool? I guess you just have to weed out the posers and imposters and find out for yourself. Maybe I'll stick around, go back towards Chinatown and go shop with the best of them. It takes a lot; a lot of patience to deal with this or should I say things like this. These things take patience and godly humbleness, these things. When I say things, I mean people and places like this. When I say places I mean like New York. And when I say people I mean people like New Yorkers.

The everything addicts, addicted to everything. These people will say everything is going their way, when everyone knows it's not. The addictive personalities that will try pretty much everything. They will try it at least once. Whatever it is. Addictions are what makes the world go around; or should I say addictions are what makes the planet spin, the Earth turn on its axis, the globe twist clockwise. Addictions make people do things that they say they will never do. Addictions are what make you say that your loved ones are crazy. There is no way that I can list all of the things that addictions do, so I will quit listing. I don't know, does our world turn counter clockwise? Whichever which way it goes, all that I am saying is that without addiction or drive this shit would come to a screeching halt. Don't you think? The whole wide world would stop. I think it would, and with all the things that people desire it does not surprise me that I do not know the difference between addiction and want. I really need to explore that, or these. These or those, here or there, now or then; who really cares?

If anyone reading this knows proper grammar PLEASE CORRECT ME NOW. Grammar was never my strong point. I have always been a good speller. Most times my ass is so tight, my farts squeak and proper English plays second fiddle. They don't even stink. My farts I mean. Well they might, to some of you, but not to me. However, right now I am trying to cleanse my body and soul, so I am somewhat accurate with all of this superficial etiquette. A Super Colon Cleanse that is what I am on. It is doctor recommended. Just read the label. This cleanse is just another addiction. It may be healthy, but who really knows? The whole process is frightening. One

(cont.)

individual is supposed to take twelve pills daily? The recommended dose is four in the morning, four at midday, and four at night. I think that this is too much shitting for one man. As it were, you might as well just shit your liver. These things are potent. I think you should only take them if you are severely constipated. But I am not severely constipated and I still take them. This makes me an addict. I am addicted to gleaning the shit out of my system among other things. I'm not going to go into my other addictions yet, but there are many. I'm sorry, but you are going to have to keep reading about my dietary supplements.

Or better yet, let me tell you about some of the stories in my court appointed alcohol and drug education class. There is a girl sitting two people away from me just itching. Itching for another taste of the lady. H, heron, smack, heroin whatever you want to call it, it is one drug I have never tried, and I'm in here for some minor DWI, DUI shit and this bitch has a major addiction to the worst possible drug. Then there's the pill poppin' Vicodin, Oxycodone addict middle aged man, and you can't forget the young coke fiend bitch over there. I guess I'm here for a reason. Oh yeah, I have to be here. I have to do seventy-three plus hours and piss tests. I have to spend the next several months with these people. This is definitely enough. Or at least it should be enough to make anyone not want to be addicted to anything. But I do not believe that is possible, I mean to not be addicted to something. Cigarettes, food, television, computers, chewing tobacco, working out; I mean come on I could go on and on. I believe everybody is addicted to something, and I think that some addictions can be healthy. And that is just life. As far as I'm concerned no life, no addiction. Chew on that. Humans are animals. Animals have desires, needs, and wants. I believe to live in a positive balance, we as human animals need to separate these things. However, this is not the easiest thing to do, therefore we have addiction.

This place is filthy.

seamless rarebit & the beach chickens.

So there were these chicks right?
There are always these chicks right?
Every story needs chicks.

Why the beach?
Why the eggs?
Why is the rarebit seamless?

Is the rarebit seamless because it's not Welsh?
The beach chickens love photographs as much as they love the beach.
The beach chickens have eggs so delicious and sweet.

The rarebit who, *by the way* is seamless; he loves eggs.
The rarebit is seamless because he always gets his eggs.
He collects his eggs even when out on a ledge.
He collects his eggs even when the beach rocks scrape his legs.

He collects his eggs in one smooth seamless swoop.
Then relishes in the glory of the eggs in his scoop.
And later he returns with the beach chickens back to the coop.

the blue rocket.

I hate having to take the subway. This is one of the only things that pisses me off about modern life living in New York City. BEING FROM CALIFORNIA, I never thought I would ever even live here in this metropolis. New York is the so-called greatest city in the world. Living here now, I'm starting to believe that it is the greatest city in the world. Consequently, now that I live here I cannot imagine a life where I didn't live here in the city. I think that everybody should experience living here for at least some significant amount of time. Let us get back to the hate. Specifically the hatred of the daily commute on the subway. To fully understand we have to go back to the place where I grew up. I grew up in San Diego, CA "The Mecca of Skateboarding." San Diego was the destination for many skateboarders across the world in the eighties and nineties, but since then there are other cities in California (SF and now LA specifically) that are considered meccas of skateboarding. With that said, the afore mentioned cities are where smooth streets, clean wide smooth sidewalks, and every type of car, from Ferraris to Honda Civics, is seen and everybody drives. You pretty much have to drive. That is, to have a productive life in Southern California from LA to SD, you must drive or at least have a friend who drives because everything is so spread out. Here, in New York City such is not the case. Here, many people have never driven in their entire lives; people well above age sixteen and even people into their old age have never even driven! For them, it's all about public transportation e.g. subways, taxicabs, ferries, and buses. And with public transportation other people control how and when the passengers get places. When I first moved out here to New York, I avoided the trains like one would avoid a hooker with the HIV. I just mean I did not want to have anything to do with them. Except for maybe to look at one (a train) with an awesome burner on it. So after a month or two I bought the quintessential "New York City car." It was a 1981 Pontiac Grand Prix LJ with a V8 engine, the kind of car DeNiro would drive in a Scorsese film. I paid $800.00 cash. I bought it from a generic gas station in Valley Stream, Long Island. It was blue. The exterior was light blue, and the interior was navy. It was beautiful except for the rust. It was very comfortable to drive and when I test drove it, I knew it was mine. It had so much potential. I knew it could be a sick nasty lowrider, or even a classic muscle car. I mean it had a V8 engine with only 113,000 miles on it and it ran like a dream. I dunno about you, but I think a car with 113,000 miles on it is pretty good, especially when it is older than some of the kids I know. I drove my car around the city everyday. It became my way to work. I even was a black market cabbie with it. I would charge the people I worked with $3.00 for a ride home each day. You know that's a good deal considering a gallon of gas is more than that nowadays plus I never had to pay for my beers. Anyway, let's get back to the look of the car. It had the look of a car that would have been in the movie "Bad Lieutenant" or "Mean Streets." The body style was totally 80's, similar to a Buick Regal, Oldsmobile Cutlass Supreme, or a Chevy Monte Carlo. It was like those cars, only beefier. I've never seen those cars with a V8. It was all stock original parts, stock rims and no crazy accessories, but this car had survived many harsh winters. You could tell by the ashy, fading, peeling paint on the trunk and the rust on the side panels and the bumper. However, all of those things are what made this car have character. I knew that car really did have character, so much that it got street casted by a producer. It got casted for an independent New York film and I rented it to the producer for $100.00 an hour. I definitely got my money's worth when it comes to how much I paid for it and how much I got out of it. It's gone but I think it's in good hands now… how I sold it is whole 'nother story.

the silence is killing me.

The silence is killing me, I can hear all the dead souls.
They are living, but they're still dead.
The silence is killing me, I'm used to listening to music;
I gotta have somethin' to fill the silent void, I mean like the T.V.
Some kind of ancillary noise that takes away from the pure thought.
But the pure thought is something. It's something...
The pure thought is something that needs to be cherished,
Because when you have the pure thought it seems like;
Nothing else is in existence, and if nothing else is in existence
Then, the silence wouldn't be killing me.
The silence is killing me...
And it is because I can't UHH! Listen to the music right now.
And uh,
It's like somebody wants me to stifle it.
And uh.
I put it on my headphones, they want me to put my headphones on.
But, if you put your headphones on...
You put your headphones on when you are at the grocery store,
The bodega or the corner store, en la izquierda, LA ESQUINA!!!
The corner you put those on...
You put those headphones on when you're on the train, the plane,
Even sometimes in the automobile...
You don't put the headphones on that much at your desk, in your house,
In your living room, unless you feel that the music should only be heard by you.
That is to say, what I just said was...
It's an isolation thing.
I'm used to hearing sounds and mostly having it on...
The secondary noise of the T.V.
The buzz of the refrigerator.
The steam of the heat pipe.
Which is sometimes called a radiator; in a hotel or in an...
Apartment in New York.
But those radiators, sometimes they make a lot of noise.
So you have that ancillary noise.
And sometimes I find myself competing...
With the noise of the radiator or the "heat pipe" as I like to call it.
With the television I try to max it out.
And maybe that deafens my hearing.
I don't know...
I like to have music, I like to have thought.

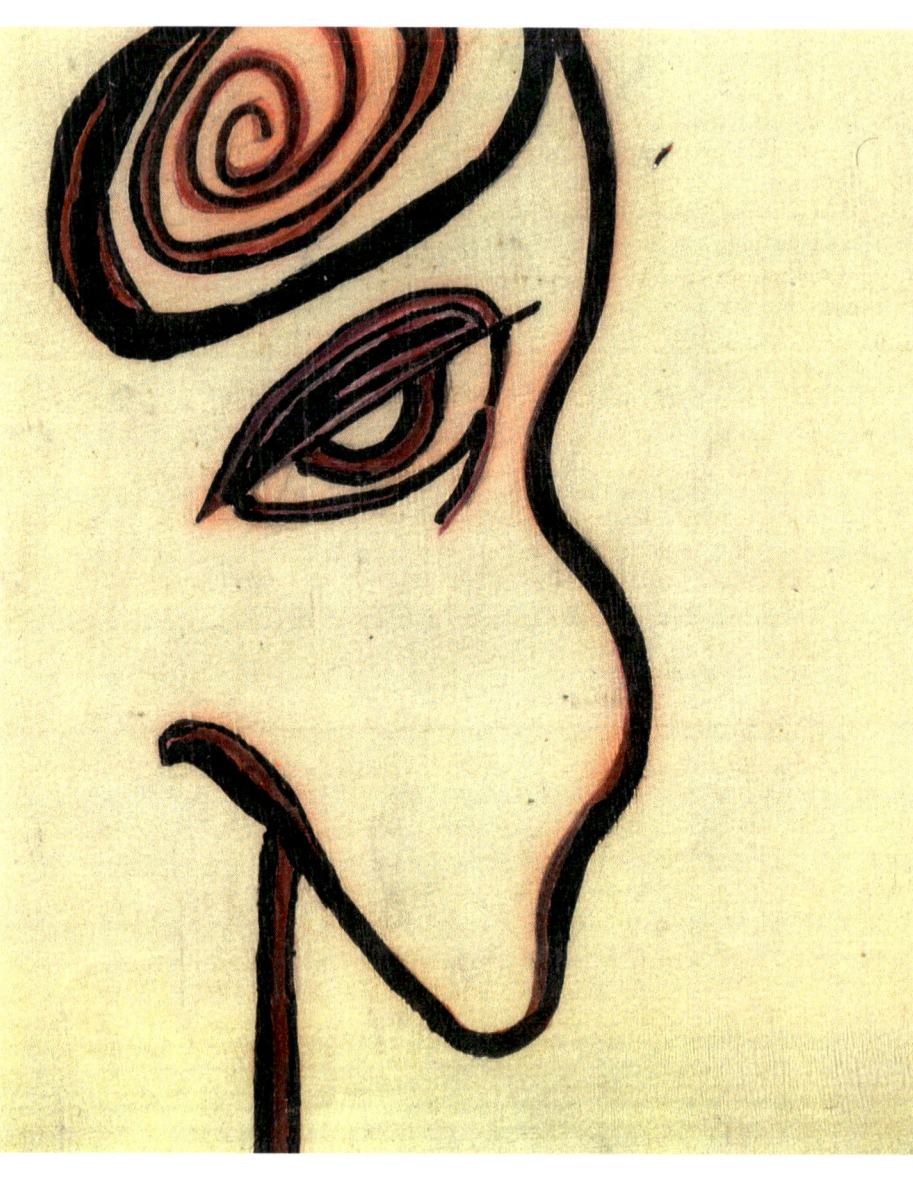

uptown scenario.

SCENARIO 1 : Open to a scene where a teen is laughing hysterically. A close-up shot on his face. He just took a huge hit, pull, puff, or whatever you call it off a can of computer dust-X, while he has the current ultra-funny Jud Apatow comedy movie on his laptop. He has an alternative soundtrack playing. It is a rawkus scene, full on physical comedy, the kind that makes you feel it when you laugh. Which is all great but this kid is feeling that and altogether a whole 'nother high induced by inhalants. We exit this scene zooming out from the 100% zoomed in can of dust-X. Fade to black.

SCENARIO 2 : The teen is a computer nerd, specifically in the digital technical media field. He is a young, smart, advanced kid who already sees and views the world as an adult. We open to him retouching a photo. The can of dust-X is not far. He is in his parent's fancy New York apartment. It is morning. He needs to make it to school on time, but he is getting high and running late because he is so into what he is retouching and he gets deeper and deeper into it after each hit. Fade out.

SCENARIO 3 : Our student arrives at his posh private school. It is the upper echelon of Manhattan. He is late. His teacher looks at him disgustingly and turns back to her lesson. He is confident, but at the same time a bit paranoid, so he takes his seat cockily to overcompensate for being high. He is smart, however he loathes conventional learning. This is a modern classroom but this particular teacher still uses a traditional black board. She writes in chalk and she uses a can of dust-X to clean it. Our student lusts for a taste of her cans. Fade out.

SCENARIO 4 : He is an only child. We are in the family apartment. We open to a tight shot of the family portrait, then pan across all the other trophy photos and accolades of our teen's parents. We scope out another hallway wall and it is filled with pictures of our teen. It is a complete chronology of his history, from baby steps to modern day. Our teen is walking out of school, through the subway, on the train, and across avenues. He is solemn.

SCENARIO 5 : He walks into the apartment. His head is down, and his backpack is weighing him down. After shedding his backpack he runs straight into the bathroom and uses it. Number two and it is a dire situation. It hit him fast, as soon as he walks in and he needs to go, badly. Next he checks his email, reads a superficial one and returns it superficially. We pan across to the can of dust-X which is always nearby.

SCENARIO 6 : He takes a huge hit on his can of dust-X, and empties it. After the high fades he tries it again, and he gets nothing. This pisses him off. He yells, "FUCK!!!" Next thing you know he is walking down the street to the office supply store.

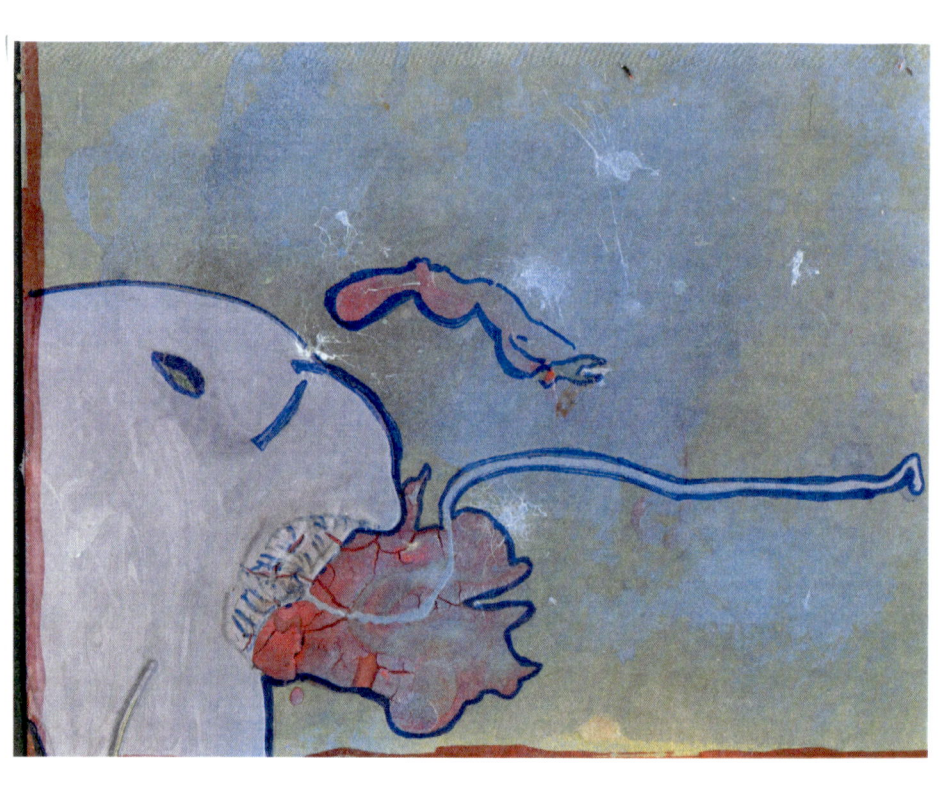

where the worms go to die.

Righteous! This is it. All in all. Dirt, life, dirt. The Earth, "The World" as we know it. Existence. Extinction. Sometimes I wake up and they are already there. Most times I wake up and you are not here. It seems that you like to tell me that you will always be there. But, most times I wake up, they are there and you are not. Who's there? Is it a woo? Is it a who? Is it a woo-who? Next time the thoughts come flooding, you had better know if it is a who, a woo, a who-woo, or some other kind of specter. There is always some kind of specter involved. That is to say, "a specter that is adhered to another sector." If there really is another sector to "The World" as we know it, please let me know and such specters in turn will be eradicated accordingly. Accordingly to Garp? No, accordingly to whatever their crime was. So listen to this, if the crime fits punish them. Punish them accordingly. They knew the rules, and then they broke them. IN-TENTIONALLY! If one breaks the rules especially if they already know them, then and only then, THEY SHALL BE PUNISHED!!! ERGO… They will visit a surreal place, a mythical place where the worms go to die.

white sands motel.

There is a motel in Las Vegas, Nevada called "White Sands Motel." It is a decrepit, downtrodden, dumpy, out of business trailer park motel squatted in by an awesome old gold-miner lookin' bastard. The crazy thing about this place is that it is right on the STRIP! It is on Las Vegas BLVD right across from the famed Luxor Hotel and Casino, the pyramid of the strip. It is the closest thing to the Egyptian Pyramids and the Egyptian desert that many will ever see. However, the real reason I'm writing about this place is the empty pool in the parking lot.

I noticed it on my way back to the Luxor after copping a twelver of Miller High Life. At first, I didn't even notice the thing had already been skateboard proofed by a shitload of rocks and debris on the floor of the shallow end and deep end. I wanted to skate it anyway so I asked the old timer if he knew where I could get a skateboard, and he said, "Git the hell outta here!" And I said, "Dude you are sitting on a gold mine right here. With this empty pool you could have the first skateboard casino on the strip." Then I asked him if I could take his picture and he said, "NO!" but I took his picture anyway.

Greetings All,

    With hardcore skateboarding (all that goes with that), writing lyrics, and dreaming since about the age of thirteen, I have developed a do it, make it, land it, stick it approach to all of the things that I do in life.

    It is amazing how these things and the images plus words that I have encountered along the way have resonated with me. Fundamentally, these things have shaped the way that I draw, paint, and write. As I focus and reflect on the gravity of all these aspects, it is no wonder that I have "Open Through the Mindflow" inside of my cranium. Additionally, don't fret I still have these kinds of original thoughts, stories, and images entering into my phrontistery daily.

Thank you, and don't forget to "OTTMF".

Genuinely, Profoundly, Wholeheartedly,

John Reeves

thank YOU's

The Reeves and extended family Matthew, Elwyn, Regina, Vanessa, Andrea, Kelly, Raymond Allen Coburn, Matt, Mariah, Marty, Raven, Alexis, Naiah, Chaz, Brian, Cianna, Frances Bournes aka F.F.B. Uncle Freddy, Auntie Gwen, Greg, Leta, Uncle Larry, Aunt Margarett, Marky, Kenyetta, my two brand new baby nephews Max and Isaiah, The Kaiser family, Marissa, Cathy, Lukas, Vera, and Allan. Jeff and Brooke Sanders.

Flolm SK8S, Dave Lively, Joe Garcia, Phil Flood, Steve Tran, John Sapienza, Jimmy Edquilang, Mike Alzona, Rick Perez, Willy Santos, Kien Lieu, Danny Minnick, Jason Carney, Huy Lee, Mikey Chin, Theo Simeon, Mike Estes, Ryan Schad, Chris Valle, Ben Arguello, Chad Vogt, Erik Salcido, Bobby and Carl at Tribal Gear, Jim and Sam at Pacific Drive, Elizabeth Johnston, Rachel Lena Esterline, Mark Gonzales, Andy Warhol, Jean-Michel Basquiat, Jackson Pollack, Shepard Fairey, Henry Rollins, Mike Vallely, David McHenry, Natas Kaupas, Steve Caballero, Tommy Guerrero, Ray Barbee, Bryce Kanights, Steve Steadham, Tony Alva, Andy Howell, Mike Giant, H-Street, Life, Invisible, Tony Magnusson, Mike Ternasky, Matt Hensley, Steve Ortega, Brian Lotti, Sal Barbier, Colby Carter, Ron Allen, Jesse Neuhaus, Dave Bergthold, Laban Pheidias, Brian Young, Joe and Susan Raia, Grant Brittain, Dave Swift, Ako and Atiba, Ted Newsome, Alex Corporan, Harold Hunter, Dave Ortiz, Adrian Lopez, Dustin Charlton, Rockstar Bearings, Max Fish, Tino, Marc, The Razo Brothers, Ivory, Shelter, The Serra Brothers, Harry Jumonji, Andy Kessler, Spencer Fujimoto, Leo Fitzpatrick, Amy @ KCDC, Jimi Hendrix, Jim Morrison, Peter Tosh, Bob Marley, Bruce Lee, Charles Bukowski, Jack Kerouac, Bad Brains, Josh Friedberg, Rick Howard, Mike Carroll, Eric Koston, Sam Smythe, Tim Gavin, The Tershay Brothers Joey and Nick, MYG, Ronnie Bertino, John Falahee, TWS, Thrasher, Big Brother, Poweredge, the Skateboard Mag, Skateboarder Magazine, For the Krew, Focus, Allen Ying, Artefuse, Bryce Ward, Bodega Skateboards, Tracker Trucks, Oscar Wagenbulcher, Max Dufour, Dayne Brummet, Peter Deller, Jaime Martinez, Joe Humeres, Quim Cardona, Ryan Zimmerman, The Witches Brew Crew, Autumn Bowl, Brian Kelley, The House of Vans BK crew, Dan Connelley, Oil City Skate Park, Richard Kenvin, A-Ron the Dowtown Don, Dan Colen, Catherine Fulmer, Casper Adams, Aura Friedman, Charles Shedden, Jerry Hsu, Maurice Sendak, Spike Jonze, D.A. Wallach, Max Drummey, William S. Burroughs, Stanley Kubrick, Hunter S. Thompson, Karri Landolfi, Greyboy, Rattyhead, Zak Najor, Dave Duncan, Choppy Omega, Don and Danielle Bostick, Christian Alfaro, Christian Hosoi, Paul Collins, James Chang, Rodger Brown, Anna Hieronymus, Neil Fenton, Josh Laurits, Tato Feliciano, Sloan Laurits, K.T. Auleta, Jason Rogers, James Frazier, Jordan Richter, Tas Pappas, Chad Muska, Harif Guzman, Crystal Moselle, Wyatt Neuman, Jena Cordova, David Foote, Harry Bee, Lurker Lou, Quim Cardona, Nicole Ianello, Ed and Deanna Templeton, Primo and Diane Desiderio, Dave Crabb, Christy King, Mike Brooke, Kate Teare, Mike McCarthy, Al and Amanda Partanen, Janine Maryam Tu, Jaymeer, Josh Falk, Glen Patricio, Jason Castaneda, Stimy from Clairemont, the whole Ericson crew, Scott Obradovich, Ron Lemen, Earle Lyons, Burnside, Washington Street, and all the homies who created those parks. Thanks to whoever I missed and a Special Thanks the Worldwide Skateboard Nation and to all whoever sponsored or supported me.